Russian
Black Magic

RUSSIAN BLACK MAGIC

The Beliefs and Practices
of Heretics and Blasphemers

NATASHA HELVIN

Destiny Books
Rochester, Vermont

Destiny Books
One Park Street
Rochester, Vermont 05767
www.DestinyBooks.com

Destiny Books is a division of Inner Traditions International

Cataloging-in-Publication Data for this title is available from the Library of Congress

ISBN 978-1-62055-887-4 (print)
ISBN 978-1-62055-888-1 (ebook)

Printed and bound in the United States

10 9 8 7 6 5 4 3

Text design and layout by Debbie Glogover
This book was typeset in Garamond Premier Pro with Garth Graphic Std, Old Russian, Gill Sans MT Pro, and ITC Legacy Sans Std used as display typefaces

To send correspondence to the author of this book, mail a first-class letter to the author c/o Inner Traditions • Bear & Company, One Park Street, Rochester, VT 05767, and we will forward the communication, or contact the author directly at **info@worldofconjuring.com**.

CONTENTS

INTRODUCTION   What Is Slavic Black Magic?   1

1   The Birth of Russian Black Magic   3

2   Veretnics and the Demonic Faith   14

3   The Demonic Pantheon   24

4   The Three Forces, the Soul, and Satanism   39

BLACK MAGIC SPELLWORK

5   Basic Rules and Principles of Magic   60

6   Principles of Cemetery Magic   85

7   Cemetery Spells   94

8   Principles of Church Sorcery   123

9   Church Spells   128

10   Blood Magic   139

11   Pact with the Devil   143

12   The Thirteen Veretnic Spells of Evil   150

Index   159

About the Author   169

INTRODUCTION

WHAT IS
SLAVIC BLACK MAGIC?

Slavic black magic is a system of ancient sorcery that originates with the black mages of Kievan Rus (Ukraine, Belarus, and Russia in 882–1240). Those mages, whose ancient spells were mostly destructive, were called black practitioners.

Sometime after the violent baptism of Russia (990–991) into the Orthodox faith, a new tradition based on old-world witchcraft began to take form. Initially it consisted of secret knowledge transmitted through notebooks wrapped in black covers and written at night. This led to it being called black magic among the common people. By association, practitioners who preserved and passed on their knowledge by recording it in the so-called black books began to be called black mages. This tradition was born about a century ago; up until then, knowledge about sorcery was mainly transmitted orally.

The echoes of ancient witchcraft practices are at the heart of modern black magic. This includes, in particular, work with the forces of nature and the world of the dead. Elements of the Christian faith were also imposed from the outside (the concepts of good and evil, God and the devil), intertwined with pagan elements. In black magic, Russian methods of sorcery are intermingled with various foreign ones. The best ones are centuries old and passed on by many generations of mages who

1

devoted themselves to the secrets of sorcery. These mages made a contract with the devil. In the process they renounced God, their families, and the forces of good. In making this contract, mages signed away their souls. In exchange, they received knowledge and power that allowed them to mediate among worlds and people, to gain various otherworldly powers, and to be masters of the natural elements. These abilities gave mages the power to control people's destinies.

The purpose of this book is to present the theories behind Russian black magic. In addition, a considerable number of practical rituals are given as illustrative examples. This book gives details concerning the secrets of cemetery and black magic rituals. Unfortunately, this book cannot provide the reader with the knowledge, rituals, experience, skills, practice, or anything else that only personal training can give. It contains only a small part of the knowledge and rituals involved. This book does not teach you how to be a mage but only partially reveals the secret knowledge that a mage possesses. It is enough for you, the reader, to understand that, with the help of sorcery, you can redirect life on the worldly plane in a way that suits you, whether that be positive or negative.

In this book I will present the foundations of the belief system and occult practiced by blasphemers and heretics. The text considers the main components of the faith: questions about the forces and people's relationships with them, the creation of the world, moral values, religious practices, attitudes toward various social institutions, and so on. The purpose of this book is to familiarize all those who are interested in the teachings of Russian black mages as it has been passed on through mage communities for generations.

1

THE BIRTH OF
RUSSIAN BLACK MAGIC

Magic is a special kind of energy. To split a rock with a hammer, you must raise and lower the hammer many times with force. In other words, you have to allocate and use energy. It is this energy that destroys the rock, not the hammer. That energy comes from your arm and hand. Magic is something like this energy, but it comes from your mind.

We must remember that society and religion have conditioned and instructed many of us about what is right and what is wrong, what is real and what is false—almost to the point that we have forgotten a fundamental truth: all life is full of mystery, and the only way to understand it is to learn about the mystery. We can search for a better understanding of what is really happening. A better understanding of the energies around us will allow us to manipulate them in such a way that our or someone else's life is positively or negatively affected. Occultism is the study of hidden, mysterious, and paranormal phenomena. It consists of many elements in life: one is the spirit, another is the universe, and a third wonderful example is consciousness.

Witchcraft is a system of certain theoretical and practical knowledge based on universal laws. Individuals with this knowledge are usually called mages. This system of knowledge enables mages to influence others. There are many different systems of witchcraft in the world, but likely the most well known and effective is the witchcraft tradition that has developed over the past two millennia based on Christianity, the world's dominant religion. At the heart of this witchcraft tradition is the confrontation between good and evil (God and the devil).

Ancient magical techniques and methods for working with natural forces and the world of the dead are closely intertwined and have been honed and systematized for centuries by many generations of mages. Though no one can accurately determine when witchcraft originated, we can safely conclude that the tradition began a long time ago. However, it was only a few centuries ago that mages organized it into a precise system, and with the spread of literacy and writing, mages began to record their knowledge on paper.

Witchcraft is not a simple craft, even if it is intended solely for oneself. It requires discipline and perseverance in achieving personal goals, constant personal growth, and self-development. Mages orally passed the black magic tradition down from generation to generation of their blood relatives. Mages who devote themselves to witchcraft as a profession do not become significantly wealthy during the course of their life. They are not allowed to become wealthy as the mages would then become lazy and quit witchcraft. But mages live, as a rule, in satiety and prosperity. If they observe the requirements of the forces that patronize them, they will be provided with all they need or, rather, with the witchcraft for obtaining the means for a decent life.

Competent mages never call themselves *magicians*. It should be noted that the word *magic* is applicable only for the circus and theatrical performances of mage-illusionists. This word is the fruit of the fantasy of various kinds of occult writers who do not have the slightest notion of either the theory or practice of witchcraft. Those who prefer to call themselves by this title are various kinds of swindlers and dilettantes; that is, white and black mages, as well as various followers of numerous homegrown secret societies and sects tailored to Western magical orders. A real expert in the field of witchcraft will never demonstrate anything in public, on a dare, or for others' curiosity, as is the lot of circus illusionists and theater mages. More precisely, this craft is called sorcery. Nowadays, it is convenient to call the spiritual work *sorcery* for the understanding of the local townsfolk. For an old specialist in witchcraft, the word *magic* sounds like an insult.

In the Russian world the word *witch* comes from the word *vedat* (meaning "know/be aware of" and "mother"). This word literally translates as "leading mother." *Witch* in Russan means "woman who has knowledge and special skills and knows how to use them."

Medieval scribes used the word *magi* to denote the biblical mages who came to the infant Jesus. It is said in the New Testament that "from the east the Magi came to Christ in Bethlehem and asked where the King of the Jews was born" (Matt. 2:1–2). In the Gospel of Matthew, the word *magi* sounds like mage, which usually means someone skilled in witchcraft. The magi (in ancient Russian the word is вълхвъ, which means "mage, fortune-teller") are a caste of Slavs who preserved ancient knowledge and applied it in practice. These are Slavic priests who performed divine services and prophesied the future.

Before Russia adopted Christianity in the tenth century, the common attitude toward mages was quite respectful. After all, these unusual people were considered intelligent and competent: they were engaged in healing and understood the forces and laws of nature. In Slavic pagan society, the mages were singled out as a special group that conducted religious rituals, prophecies, and fortune-telling. In the ancient Slavic hierarchy, the magi traditionally occupied a high place, next to the ruler. Princes came to the magi for prophecies. Mages function as spiritual mentors and intermediaries between worlds and between people and the world of invisible energy streams. A mage was considered a prophet, shaman, healer, and crafter of potions. They created curses and performed rituals for exacting retribution, beguiling someone, attracting wealth and luck, and protection, as well as concocting potions composed of various herbs and insects for causing harm, stirring up passion, and other purposes. The mages could heal, conjure, and tell the future, as well as interpret the dreams and nighttime visions of ordinary people. Many people listened to them. Almost every village had a shaman or mage that people went to for advice in difficult situations.

After Christianity was adopted, people came to fear and dislike mages; consequently, many mages do not really like people. Despite their dislike of mages, people have always turned to them for help when a problem could not be solved by traditional methods.

Since ancient times, black-magic practitioners have not been particularly friendly with one another, but they have not been at odds either, at least not openly. Bitter wars have flared up at times, however. If reconciliation between those in conflict was not possible, the stronger of the two won. In spite of this, mages often gathered in the old days for masses (mage gatherings). There they discussed their shared pressing questions and exchanged experiences. These gatherings still occur but much less often, and when they do happen, the gatherings are much more organized. Sometimes mages gather for collective ceremonies that usually include three people (most often a male mage and two female mages). Such a trio is called a braid, as a braid is usually made from three strands. Mages gather for a collective rite when it is necessary to eliminate someone by joint efforts or to achieve some other important goal. Sometimes mages gather in groups of nine or more to conduct collective rituals.

THE SUPPRESSION OF PRE-CHRISTIAN FAITHS

From the beginning of time, all cultures have had mystical traditions, secret teachings, and myths explaining the nature of the world. Many of these myths were dichotomies that divided the world into cosmic and chthonic forces: the light gods of heaven and the dark gods of the underworld. The forces of the original universe were projected onto heaven and earth and took on forms native to those places. A way to think about this is that there is a tree with two sets of branches; the first set of branches grew in heaven, and the second set grew in the underworld. Each group had its own hierarchy, fulfilled a role in the universe, and guarded secrets. Both sets of branches were made of intelligent spiritual beings—angels in the upper world, demons in the underworld—each with a name, personal characteristics, a particular form, and a seal. The different branches are all of *one* tree trunk. The different paths, spirits, and demons of witchcraft are all connected to one concept and one concept only: the manipulation and manifestation of the human will.

The Christian church conquered countries with fire and sword and united them under one Christian faith. The conquered peoples became vassals and slaves for their masters, who marched under the Christian banner of the Christian god. The Christian church gained dominance over earlier pre-Christian faiths throughout Europe, Asia, and Latin America by asserting that only faith in the Christian god was true and good. Thus proponents of the Christian faith suppressed the pagan practices of various ethnic groups and by doing so these practices assumed the role of evil. These other faiths became forbidden, their language and rituals deemed repulsive. The church insisted on indiscriminately denying the history and culture of a number of ethnic groups, which led to divisions and isolation among peoples.

The church actually helped to bring the dark force of evil into people's lives. Before the Christian era, evil went under many different names and was not relegated to a single force or entity. These various evil forces were small and sometimes associated with natural phenomena, such as thunder, rain, fire, volcanic activity, predators, and ordinary death. With the advent of Christianity, evil was attributed solely to the devil or Satan, who resided in the underworld or hell.

The names of the familiar old gods of this or that people became, under Christianity, the names of demons. Thus, according to the Christian church, all who honored the old gods began to worship demons, Satan, and the devil. As it happens, the word *demon* comes from the ancient Greek δαίμων, meaning "deity, spirit, demon," which derives from δαίω, meaning "divide, share, or distribute," and initially referred to a god who gave out destinies to people. With the arrival of Christianity this neutral or even beneficent god quickly became identified as a demon or equivalent to the devil.

Christian preachers called Satan and death the evil beginning. At first people were puzzled as to why their gods were now considered evil demons. Eventually the newly gathered parishioners began to believe that all the old gods were wicked devils, bringers of evil. Nonetheless, people continued to appeal to the old gods.

DUAL FAITH:
RUSSIAN BLACK MAGIC AND CHRISTIANITY

In the territory where the Slavs lived, Christianity combined with vedic (from the Russian *vedat*), old-world witchcraft, and so Slavic black magic was born. It differed significantly from the dark traditions of the Middle East, Asia, and Africa, and yet it had the same features of a strict belief system. Everything was reconciled in form, content, and ritual structure. This system was kept secret and known only to its initiates. Even now, Slavic mages will not risk exposing their secrets.

Slavic or Russian black magic has as its foundation dual faith. Dual faith is an exclusively Russian phenomenon; it has no equivalent in other cultures. The Russian people have never been fanatically Christian, and in Russia pagan belief systems were preserved and blended with Christianity after it was forcibly imposed. What distinguishes dual faith is not the Orthodox Christian component but the concept of an official, Christian, public faith.

The tradition of Russian black magic is primarily a system of witchcraft. But it is also a complex religious cult that worships the Unclean Forces. Mages very carefully study all the forces with which they interact. They are consciously guided by the idea that knowledge generates power. In other words, it allows them to properly direct this force and achieve conscious goals for personal development.

Black magic and sorcery encompass very broad concepts. Each magical system, of which there are many, is based on the power and omnipotence of the dark gods, hence the dark path toward spiritual evolution. In the Slavic tradition, the left-hand path is the one that leads to black magic. Russian magic is nothing more than the opposite of Orthodoxy, just as Western ceremonial magic with its black mass is the opposite of Catholicism. Although I love the Russian black magic tradition for itself, I recognize its dependence on Christianity. People were not allowed to be anything but Christian in Russia for the past thousand years, so an alternative was formed. People, in open rebellion, could choose to honor Satan instead of God, which became the basis of Russian black magic.

Practitioners of Russian black magic conjure various demons by name and read psalms for different purposes. Actually, all traditional systems, from the paganism of ancient Rus to Haitian voodoo, were not solely based on folkloric magical rites. Religious doctrine and sacral beliefs were also always part of these systems, including divination, magic, and summoning spirits. In Abrahamic religions, the role of the latter was reduced, and religious dogma was given precedence. Many sects followed the same pattern. Heresy emphasizes witchcraft and also personal ministry, such as how to solve a person's problems and fulfill his needs.

Mages work in forests, at crossroads, in swamps, on riverbanks, and with fire. The differences are visible in the rituals of black magic and Satanism. All rituals are held in dark places, where people generally do not go voluntarily, such as cemeteries, old roads, crossroads, swamps, forests, and abandoned villages. They don't engage in overt philosophizing or shocking and ostentatious anti-Christianity. As a rule, mages rarely dress in all black, do not wear flashy paraphernalia, and do not start arguments that might attract the attention of the Orthodox.

Black mages and magical artisans appeal to demons, which are the original dark gods who hold the power of destruction and chaos. The pantheon of Russian black magic consists of various legions of demons. Each legion has a senior demon, called a black prince. He has demon assistants, and each assistant in turn has demonic assistants, further down the hierarchy. A mage must necessarily have an assistant, a so-called inferior spirit who is not a soul at rest but a devil or demon. Even sorceries based on different traditions have the concept of an "assistant." In voodoo, the Bocor (voodoo warlock) traps the soul of a person who has died in a state called *govi*. This person will serve the Bocor for as long as the Bocor wants him to.

Mages (namely, female ones) are a special category of people who are in kinship or collusion with the Unclean Forces. (The differences between males and females who practice the craft is a subject for another book.) These forces either empower them with supernatural abilities from birth or endow them with a specially formed contract. Mages for the most part harm people; that is, curse them, cast love spells on people against their will, or promise people wealth in exchange for goods: traditionally, cows (or any kind of animal), food, or gold; nowadays usually money, but it depends on the area, if we are talking about rural Russia then domestic animals for food, gold, houses, or even help with fields could be exchanged. Sometimes, however, they help people in exchange for a large payment: they remove curses and spells by negotiating with the Unclean Forces.

According to popular belief, the power of a mage depends not only on individual strength but also on the number of demons that act as their patrons. Patrons guard mages from birth or are acquired in the process of becoming a mage. The demons who serve mages fulfill many of their needs and even sometimes bring them blessings in return for their souls. In addition, mages may make other trades with evil spirits for specific purposes.

TRAINING AND DISCIPLES

Mages must train disciples to replenish their ranks. Becoming a disciple of a real mage (master) is extremely difficult because mages are not willing to share their personal experiences. The quantity and quality of knowledge the learner receives depends on the abilities the initiate was born with and how he or she manifests this potential during the learning process.

There are two types of mages: ancestral mages and natural mages. From ancient times to this day, ancestral mages received or inherited their knowledge and strength from their bloodlines. Natural mages are those who received power at birth from the Unclean Force (or Satan).

Natural mages are born very rarely. They are usually called stewards or sometimes phenoms. Often they do not even need to seek out a teacher; they naturally understand the principles of witchcraft. They just need to find a mentor for a short time (an experienced mage, preferably also natural), one who will guide them and teach them the concepts and principles of witchcraft. Sometimes natural mages are self-taught. Being a natural mage is not as enviable as it might seem; having these abilities is primarily a burden. The forces impose higher demands on natural mages than on ordinary mages and also often impose certain limitations on their personal lives. Evil spirits don't absorb their souls; instead, the mages are sent into the world again and again to do the demons' bidding. They are usually not as noticeable as ordinary mages, so they are easier to overlook.

Ancestral mages train mainly for free by transferring knowledge to members of their own clan; they consider paying for the education unacceptable. (Ancestral and natural mages have gotten into fierce arguments about whether the training should be paid or free.) Depending on the circumstances, the ancestral mage may have a blood relationship with the student; members of the clan do not always share a blood relationship. Ancestral mages may also choose to transmit knowledge only to their own blood kinship over the course of their lives. Ancestral mages don't offer a partial transfer of knowledge to their students.

Natural mages who have a talent for magic from birth usually train other natural mages. In these cases, the student pays for the knowledge. Anyone with a penchant for sorcery could be a student as long as he or she pays with money or, in the past, domestic animals (cows, goats, sheep, geese, chickens) or by working for the mage. A mentor who takes on the training of a disciple transfers a part of his knowledge, experience, and personal power to the student. Payment or working serves as a restoration of the spent energy.

Both natural and ancestral mages must complete the transfer of knowledge before their death. If they do not transfer all their power, their death will be gruesome and painful. Evil spirits brutally torture a dying mage who carries untransferred knowledge to his grave. Death will only come to him after a long and terrible torment. It should be noted that a mage's magical power is not only based on what he learned during his training; a mage's power also derives from the knowledge he has accumulated over a lifetime.

In a mage's last years, he donates all his knowledge, techniques, secrets, tricks, subtleties of craft, personal achievements, communication with the forces who patronize him, and his powers to his successor. He records all the ins and outs of his craft and personal experience and passes them to the recipient of his choosing. In the presence of heirs, the information on witchcraft is passed by blood relationship; and in the absence of heirs, it is passed to a carefully selected successor from outside the clan. This complete transfer of knowledge and strength is performed by the mage at the foot of a mountain after a year to one successor and is free of charge.

Natural mages differ from experienced spellcasters in that the latter, as a rule, use their visionary capabilities to perceive the whole environment rather than individual elements. Spellcasters are people who learn to do spells. They are goal-oriented people, and they focus on how to cast successful spells, mostly for profit. Ancestral witches don't care about profit much but focus more on connection with family members, spirits, and otherworldly beings. They mediate between worlds.

2

VERETNICS AND THE DEMONIC FAITH

U pon the adoption of Christianity, the attitude toward mages became sharply negative. They were persecuted, immolated in the "sacred" bonfires of Orthodoxy. Many educated people of that time, even those who had nothing to do with witchcraft, fell before the ruthless machinations of the new dogma. The grand church did not suffer any rivals in its path. It wanted to seize control of people's minds.

One of the most well-known offshoots of the Russian mage is the Veretnics. The very name comes from the word *heretic;* that is, someone who believes differently from the accepted orthodoxy. Another root is the word *veretno,* which means "spindle"; spindles were part of initiation rites in ancient times.

Heresy

Heresy (from the ancient Greek αἵρεσις, which means "choice, direction, school, doctrine, sect") is a conscious departure from the generally accepted religious teachings. It offers a different approach to religious teachings and calls for the separation of the church from a new community. The negative meaning of the word *heresy* was first expressed in the New Testament. The logic of this transformation is that, since truth and life can be found only in Christ (John 14:6), any alternative automatically condemns a person to destruction. Accordingly, the apostle Peter speaks of "pernicious heresy" (2 Pet. 2:1), and the apostle Paul places heresies on a par with the sins of witchcraft and idolatry (Gal. 5:20). Following the example of the apostles, the early Christian church used the term *heresy* to designate a doctrine that is divorced from Christian Orthodoxy, or a group of people who broke away from the church as a result of adherence to such a doctrine.

Veretnic is a branch of Russian witchcraft that uses Christian objects and symbols to create blasphemy and destruction. Veretnics, unlike mages, do not engage in ordinary witchcraft. They worship the devil as the totality of all the Unclean Forces, and the demons as the incarnations of the devil. It is believed that Veretnics work directly with demons and specifically with the nine black princes led by Satan. Veretnic is fundamentally different from the traditions of devil worship in other countries (in the West, for example). It has its own unique system, which it did not borrow from other traditions, with rare exceptions. Veretnic is not, however, a religious sect.

Veretnics pray to Satan tirelessly, conduct various black rituals and masses, and try to destroy all life on Earth. Veretnics especially hate Christian Orthodox icons, which they desecrate. By destroying them, they try to prove the insignificance of the church and the greatness of their true master, the devil. A lot of Veretnic rituals are somehow connected with blasphemy, which gives Satan and his demonic brothers great pleasure. As a rule, rituals are performed in solitude.

The Veretnics glorify the Unclean Forces by name and read black prayers and psalms, which are contained in a hymnal psalter. This demonic psalter is not a converted Christian text but is an original educational guide containing traditional legends, such as myths about the fall of certain angels into hell and predictions of the future, when God will be cast into hell. The psalter has invocations for the devil or the Evil One, who is a single demonic essence, the collective mind of the Unclean Forces.

In general, Veretnics are considered to be the most powerful and dangerous mages because they often practice the habitation of various demons; in other words, they become possessed. It must be said, however, that their witchcraft is often of a one-sided nature. Undoubtedly some Veretnics make love charms, but mainly they cast curses. It is believed that in ancient times, namely during the baptism of Rus, some particularly zealous mages began to destroy icons, crosses, and other artifacts, and some of them, later called fierce elders by the Veretnics, received revelations from demons who told them that mockery of the shrines was like balm to the demonic soul. Many of these mages were then given special powers in addition to these revelations. Descendants of the fierce elders and their disciples began to make demonic prayers (known as blessings) and develop incantations and rites, most of which were directly associated with blasphemy. Although Veretnics have all the attributes of ordinary mages, this obsession with desecration left its mark on them. Many Veretnics report that if they do not cast spells for a long time, they have a feeling of discomfort. Some say that the Veretnics are obligated to cast curses because the demons they serve demand it and will cause them discomfort if they don't.

It is important to clearly distinguish between real mages, who help people with the knowledge that has been handed down from generation to generation, and fanatics with a sick but rich imagination who pose a threat to others. There is also a third group that includes all kinds of charlatans and swindlers who exploit human grief. It was partly thanks to scammers and people with sick psyches that the common people lost faith in healers. To protect yourself and your loved ones from harm, be sure to research a mage from whom you seek help.

Hell Icons

The Veretnics create and paint black icons depicting demons, known as hell icons. The black icon eye of the devil, one of the main hell icons, is dedicated to the Evil One.

There are numerous legends about hell icons. Though they are mentioned in different historical documents, real examples of such icons have not survived to the modern day. The term *hell icons* was first found in a sixteenth-century manuscript titled "The Life of Basil the Blessed." It describes how Basil the Blessed* went to the city gate, where there was a miraculous icon with the image of the Mother of God.

The crowd of pilgrims who surrounded the wonderful image were surprised to see that he did not pray but instead threw a stone at the icon. The saint explained that there was an image of the devil under the top layer of paint. He revealed the hidden image as proof.

Hell icons were considered especially dangerous for believers, because both the visible and hidden images were inextricably linked to one another. A Christian who prayed to an icon of a saint or Jesus simultaneously prayed to the devil. For ordinary people, this was a real test of faith. At the same time it was a sort of game to try to recognize the "devilish temptations." Hell icons were a special kind of black magic.

One explanation for hell icons is that they were created by old believers who did not accept church reform and did not want to obey the new Greek methods of worship accepted in the seventeenth century. The old believers were the ones who crafted and distributed hell icons, all to undermine the faith of the Christians who had accepted the reform.

---

*Basil the Blessed is an Orthodox Christian saint. A so-called fool for Christ and a wonder-worker, he lived in Moscow at the time of Tsar Ivan the Terrible. He is also known as Vasily, Vasily Blazhenny, Basil Fool-for-Christ, or Basil of Moscow (source: the orthodoxwiki website).

Another explanation for this phenomenon is that these icons were created by Jews seeking to confront the heresy of the official church. Jews did not accept the worship of icons. In their opinion, icons were actually idols, and worshipping them was idolatry, which contradicted the commandment "You shall not make for yourself an idol." To erode belief in holy icons, they spread the hidden hell images.

A third explanation for the creation of hell icons was the simple fraud of peddlers (merchants). One icon dealer sold an ordinary-looking icon to a buyer and left. Then another peddler came to the target and showed him the hidden layer with its devilish designs. Such a case was described by Nikolai Leskov in the story "The Sealed Angel." In 1873 the writer also published a small study of the phenomenon of hell icons.

DEMONIC DOCTRINE

A distinctive feature of the demonic faith is the absence of the strict dogmas that are common in Abrahamic religions (Christianity, Judaism, and Islam). However, all heretics share common ideas that form the basis of demonic doctrine. The paganism of ancient Rus (today Ukraine, Belarus, and Russia) was similar. Each tribe lived according to its own specific customs but shared Slavic gods, such as Veles (god of earth, waters, forests, and the underworld), Dazhbog (god of fire, sun, and rain), Perun (god of thunder and lightning), and Mokosh* (protector of women's work and destiny), were universally revered.

Tribal deities also held a place. The role of this or that local mythological character held a position below the main Slavic gods. Nevertheless the various tribes viewed the world and the nature of things in a similar way. Animism and totemism (the deification of fire,

---

*Mokosh watches over spinning and weaving and the shearing of sheep and protects women in childbirth.

water, thunder, oak) were the cornerstones of their thinking. Their gods also reflected the common social roles of the soldier, farmer, mother, and others.

Like Hinduism, the demonic faith of ancient Rus resembled an ancient river with many tributaries—various offshoots, schools, and sects. Its ideas of karma, reincarnation, and dharma were not as well developed as in Hinduism, however. Although the demonic faith, which was first formulated in the Slavic lands between the fifteenth and sixteenth centuries, has some common beliefs, mages often differ in their chosen pantheon of demons and mythological symbols.

Witchcraft and secret arts in general are associated with the phases of the moon. According to the mages, Earth holds nothing but the dead in their coffins. They are ruled over by Death, the mistress of the cemeteries. God rules in heaven and does not interfere in earthly matters, though he does try to control the increasing number of human souls.

Generally speaking, all heretical mages hold the same stance on the nature of the forces of the universe. God and his son, the devil, are like the apple tree and its fruit. Neither is inherently good nor evil. They are beings of intelligent energy who have similar goals and need humans to continue existing. They believe that the human soul is in the mind, and people are intelligent energy in shells of flesh. How a man thinks and acts will determine his path in death. A man who lives by his passions will go to the devil. A man who ignores his flesh and his natural needs, who wishes to erase his ego and quickly become one with the divine light, will be absorbed by God. It's no wonder that Satan is called the prince of this world. Whoever lives in worldly ways will spend his afterlife in Earth.

Another shared belief among adherents of the demonic faith is the creation and purpose of mankind. In black prayers, it is clear that God is no better than the devil. The only difference is that the devil is more willing to help people because he lives in exile. He wants to accumulate power and so is interested in all new souls. In addition, the demons have long established themselves in natural spaces and underground kingdoms. They therefore have full access to the riches of Earth. They inhabit the elements and have absorbed them into themselves. God cannot help with these earthly matters, nor does he need to. He already holds the throne.

It's possible to repay the devil in various ways. Some heretics work for specific demons in the demonic pantheon, while others do not recognize the different entities. They invoke evil spirits in simple terms and refer to that collective force only as the devil or the demon. Most heretics have hell icons to pray over and use in witchcraft.

The ancient religion of Slavic paganism was heavily related to the forces of nature. By worshipping the primordial deity, a person could touch the mysteries of the universe and control the forces of nature.

Black magic as a full-fledged system of witchcraft was created at the time of the dual faith, after the violent baptism of Kievan Rus. Belobog and Chernobog kept the world balanced: the white god Belobog of light and sun was the counterpart of the dark and cursed god Chernobog. These gods were on equal footing until Russia was forcibly baptized into the Christian faith. Then Chernobog became a demon with horns and hooves (which, as it happens, represent the forces of nature!). Russian black magic is characterized by its universality and adaptations to Slavic culture. Beliefs varied slightly from one mage to the next based on where each was located.

Occult actions are called rituals among those who are knowledgeable. A ritual includes an action, a spell, and a mental representation in the mind of the intended result of the action and spell. There are rituals that consist of only the spell and the mental representation of the intended action, such as curses, the evil eye, hexes, and charms. Rituals are not meaningless actions paired with any string of words. Each action and word used in a ritual is carefully chosen based on certain principles to achieve the intended result. These principles are based mainly on the laws of physics.

Spells are verbal representations that can be adapted as desired. The spells used in the rites are associated with the actions performed in the rites. A spell helps to concentrate and aim forces on a given goal. The effectiveness of the actions of a curse (as well as of all rituals) usually depends on the object of worship or an egregor* and also from the personal power of the person who casts the spell. Often, however, the spell and ritual actions are based only on the personal power of the one performing the ritual.

THE INTERSECTION OF MAGIC AND RELIGION

The teachings of heretics are closely connected with the belief that it is possible to influence the world through an appeal to otherworldly forces. A heretic is a mage who forms a contract with the Unclean Forces. It can be said that a heretic is an Eastern Slavic mage with pronounced elements of anti-Christianity, which arose in folklore. From very early on, they were known as wise and learned. In fact, any nonmonotheistic religion is closely related to magic and intersects with others, with some regional differences. These include shamanism (veneration of the spirits of wind, fire, the forces of the underworld, and ancestors) or, for example, voodoo, where work is done with the help of a variety of powers, such as the *loa,* Haitian voodoo gods or masters of forests, rivers, or the afterlife. They also include modern paganism and Wicca. Witchcraft and shamanic rituals are regularly performed by members of the priestly estate, such as shamans, houngans (voodoo priests), priests, and druids, for ordinary believers. These are celebrations of the annual cycle. No tradition is purely magical or purely religious. To be completely honest, even Christianity, which prohibits magic, had elements

---

*Egregor is an occult concept representing a thoughtform or collective group mind, an autonomous psychic entity made up of and influencing the thoughts of a group of people. It is an energy form endowed with consciousness.

of genuine necromancy (reverence of the relics, storage of parts of the deceased, prayers to the dead or to saints) and magic (cutting a lock of hair, dipping into the font, turning to this or that side of the world) in its rites, and marks of this can even be found in the architecture of churches. *Heresy* is, in fact, a magical term. In it, the otherworldly forces are the most important element of the whole dogma, although the practice of witchcraft is not actually required. Heretics honor forces in their habitats—forests, fields, rivers, cemeteries, swamps, and so on. Nevertheless, there are ritual actions associated with various offerings to, for example, the master of the forest and the mistress of cemeteries, which the majority of heretics perform. They receive real help from the forces in earthly matters and spiritual searches.

Heretics are often criticized for opposing Christianity. But how can it be otherwise, when the religion that dominates our land was fostered in Russia for political reasons a thousand years ago? The followers of Christianity defame demons in every way, distorting the truth about the origin of humanity and of souls, supporting lies about the nature of God as a supposedly omnipotent know-it-all, and frightening ignorant people with terrible stories about eternal torments in hell. Interestingly, the threat of hell is combined with the idea of God as the source of love and good.

And yet the source of this omnipotence is invisible. In the Book of Exodus there is the phrase "No one has seen God at any time." Have you yourself seen the Lord God, the Heavenly Father, or even Jesus except as an image? Christians worship entities who are invisible. During the millennia of the church's history, God has not appeared to any mortal. Heretics do not worship invisible gods hiding from them in the pages of dogmatic writings. Nor do they call for all to believe blindly in an authority, such as the pope, who dreams of angelic tabernacles under the euphoric music of the church organ and who, incidentally, has never seen his master, any more than his predecessors have.

Demonic forces are clearly present alongside us and can come in a visible form. This is not a question of faith or religion; anyone who wants to establish contact with demons sees this. The simplest examples are the master of the forest and the demons, ghouls, and various evil spirits described in folklore. Thousands of instances of proof can be found in ethnographic studies. We do not need dogmatic faith or academic knowledge to be sure of the existence of these forces.

3

THE
DEMONIC PANTHEON

At the head of the demonic pantheon are the nine great demon princes: Satan, Veligor, Versaul, Aspid, Enoch, Enarh, Death, Indik, and Mafawa. The demonic pantheon as a whole—that is, the amalgamation of demonic power—is usually called the devil. The leaders of the princes, also known as the devil's trinity, are Satan, Veligor, and Versaul. The devil's trinity is headed by the great Prince Satan. All of them are fallen angels who earlier served as assistants to God in heaven and performed various tasks on his orders. But one day they started a riot to remove God from the heavenly throne. After the fierce battle ended, God cast them down to Earth, or rather into its bowels. There they were reborn as demons.

PRINCE SATAN

The devil's principalities are ruled by the great Prince Satan, also known as the fallen angel Satanel. He is the eldest son of God and his right hand. He initially performed certain cruel tasks at God's behest. He, like many other angels who fell from the heavens, helped his father and took direct part in the creation of man. Satanel, after raising the rebellion, was rejected by his father and cruelly punished for all eternity.

He was cast down from heaven and given the name Satan; he lost the angelic suffix *-el*.* When God cast Satanel from the skies and into Earth, the fallen angel struck the surface so deeply that he settled in its bowels next to the Pit of Fire in a lake of magma. This was the underworld, or hell. Eight more once-majestic fallen angels were cast down after him, along with a great many assistants. All of them turned into demons in their new living conditions in Earth's fiery core.

Because he fell first, Satan settled deeper than all the others in the depths of Earth. The others who followed established their principalities in the bowels of Earth. The demons took their places in a hierarchy based on the order of their fall. Together they formed the nine circles of hell (or rather, these circles were at the threshold of hell itself), or the nine great principalities. To prevent the demons from escaping hell and starting a new battle for the heavenly throne, God placed his sword—the sun—over Earth. Because of this, the demons and the rest of the lesser demons can only awaken at night. That amount of time is not enough to reach heaven and begin a new battle.

The name Satan means "opposing"; that is, confronting God. His army is constantly striving to reestablish Satan on Earth by swaying people to his side. Satan is clever, strong, and cruel. He tricks people he considers two-faced. It is not easy to get his patronage. He gives it only to those who are truly loyal to him. Mages appeal to Satan and give their souls in exchange for his protection in sorcery and worldly life. However, many natural mages do not need to do this because they are under his patronage from birth. Ordinary people must consciously stand by his side and make a contract with him. He can give them health, wealth, luck, success, protection, and so on, according to their wishes. In legend, Satan has the appearance of a giant muscular man with an animal's face, hooves for feet, horns on his head, and webbed

---

*Satan is also Saturn (Cronus in Greek) and the Hindu god Shiva. Slavs call him Dia-vol (meaning "Marvelous Bull"). He is the Golden Taurus, he is Zeus, he is Jupiter, and he is Perun among the Slavs.

wings on his back. His body is covered with thick fur, but he can change his appearance endlessly, just as other demons can. He prefers to spend most of the night on Earth's surface. He descends to its depths only in the daytime, when he must hide from the sunlight.

Satan is surrounded by his closest assistants, the demons Herod and Pilate, and a huge army of lesser demons. It is these demons whom he contracts to mages as personal patrons. One of his closest assistants is Herod, his son, who is commonly called the Antichrist and sometimes Lucifer. The other is Pilate. They are surrounded in their turn by their closest assistants. Many novice mages, self-taught, try to learn from Satan himself in various ways, but this is stupid and not safe because Satan does not teach anyone himself. His numerous assistants are the ones who bestow knowledge.

Herod has demon Abar as his assistant; Abar is commonly called the church demon and is a sort of demonic mutant, a kind of twisted messenger. He is able to cross on to holy ground without pain. According to legend, Satan assigned the young demon a task, but he couldn't cope with it and was afraid to return to Satan's side. So he went to church, asking God to protect him from Satan's wrath. God took pity on Abar, and he settled permanently in churches. Later, though, he was drawn to evil deeds again. He was, after all, a demon. He began to help those who appealed to him in churches for a small fee in the form of inverted church candles and blasphemous temples praising him. In the afternoon, he behaves modestly and works mainly in the early darkness. In churches where no one appeals to him, he is extremely weak, and he often abandons those churches. In churches where he is often approached, he awakens and gains strength and power.

The demon Pilate is surrounded by the following assistants: demon Amodeus and demoness Herodian. Herodian is commonly called the breeder. She is the wife of Satan and mother to the demon Herod. She came from the soul of Lilith, the first woman and first wife of Adam, who did not want to live with him because of her rebellious streak and violent temperament (she was killed for her excessive lasciviousness and disobedience of God's orders). The twelve daughters of the demon Herod and the demoness of death are well known, but they do not have a direct relationship with the first demonic army. They are under their mother's wing, despite the fact that they tend to roam all over Earth to harass the human race. Therefore we will describe them below, since they relate to the seventh demonic army.

PRINCE VELIGOR

The second in the pantheon is the great Prince Veligor. Initially he, not Satan, was God's first assistant in heaven. He held a very high position in the heavenly hierarchy of the angels. After God replaced him with Satanel, Veligor harbored a fierce grudge against God. In fact, he was the first to incite a rebellion in heaven by urging Satanel to act. Veligor was the second to be cast from heaven into the depths of Earth, after Satan. He became the embodiment of evil. Veligor is one of the most powerful and evil demons because it was his destiny to bear evil from birth. Veligor likes to appear beautiful before people and enchant them with smooth speeches. He beguiles them to sinful deeds, evil, and depravity. In the hierarchy of demons, he has great power. He is deceitful and treacherous. He often does not fulfill his promises, but he does patronize mages who are truly devoted to him and therefore deserving of his favor. He is generous to those he chooses. He loves offerings in the form of fire and blood sacrifices. Veligor prefers to remain in the depths of hell and only periodically ascends to Earth's surface to foment evil. His true appearance is that of a giant black wasp with shaggy paws and the face of a half beast, half man. He transforms into various beautiful forms to better manipulate humans.

Prince Veligor is flanked by his closest assistants, demons Arzhun and Korzhak, who were created in his likeness. He also has a huge army of many lesser demons, which he provides to mages as personal patrons.

The demon Arzhun is an invincible warrior. He is strong, clever, cunning, and treacherous. He has two assistants at his side: demons Rahab and Cain. Cain, son of Eve and Prince Aspid, is half demon, half man.* The rebellious angels, when they were still in heaven, arranged for Adam's second wife, Eve, to be seduced by Aspid. The angels were thus able to teach the first people to enjoy sexual intercourse and bring the birth of humans (and the production of souls) outside God's control.

Many descendants born from liaisons with earthly males were also created by the aforementioned demoness Herodian. It is believed that in many people there is a particle of the blood of Cain and Herodian. This bloodline bestows mages with the natural gift of sorcery.

PRINCE VERSAUL

Third in the pantheon of the demons of Russian black magic is the great Prince Versaul. He was a member of the council of angels in heaven. At Satanel's first appeal, he went to his side and took part in the rebellion against God. He was also cast down to Earth by God as a result and turned into a demon. He is strong and powerful. He likes to patronize mages loyal to him, just as he loves to patronize the gatherings of mages. He prefers to appear before them in the guise of a strong and tall man, black as a Moor, with a menacing face, horns on his head, and wings on his back. But his true appearance is an ugly black fly with spider legs and an ugly human face; he moves about with the help of huge wings. He prefers to spend most of his time flying around on Earth's surface. He retreats to Earth's bowels or to the dark thickets of a forest whenever he needs to hide from sunlight.

---

*Cain is the eldest son of Adam and Eve. In kabbalah, he is the son of the angel Samael and Eve, or, in gnosticism, the son of the Unclean One (Satan) and Eve, the first man born on Earth. He is the first murderer, who deprived his brother Abel of life. The name Cain comes from the Hebrew word *qayin,* which means "to acquire or possess."

Versaul also has a huge army of lesser demons, whom he provides to mages as personal patrons.

PRINCE ASPID

The fourth in the pantheon is the great Prince Aspid. He also entered the council of angels in heaven and was the second to answer Satanel's call to take part in the uprising against God. According to legend, Aspid is considered to be Satan's nephew. Along with the other rebellious angels, he was cast down to Earth and became a demon.

Before the rebellion in heaven, Aspid felt the wrath of God for seducing Eve. Aspid has a long dragonlike body with a human head and a terrible mouth; he has webbed wings, short paws, and a long tail. He dwells in great expanses of water but periodically ascends to the surface of Earth to perform his evil deeds. Aspid is the demon of greed and envy. He likes to urge people to sins and actions that are contrary to the worship of God. Aspid, like the other demons, has close associates, as well as a huge army of other lesser demons.

Aspid controls all the evil spirits of all the expanses and depths of water. He is commonly known in the Old Slavic tradition as the demon of water. It is believed that he can be seen in the daytime and can appear as an old man, covered with moss, mud, and marsh grass, but much larger than an ordinary man. He can also be covered with gray hair and have horns on his head or take the shape of a huge catfish. But like any other demon, he can assume any shape he likes. He likes to travel, accompanied by his assistants, to the depths of the sea and into the ruins of flooded cities and villages. It is believed that he and his assistants drown beautiful young women. He later brings these women to live with him, transforming them into demonesses. They, in turn, seek human souls by luring men into water and drowning them. Sailors, rivermen, fishermen, and millers with water mills who were fortunate, their businessses thriving, were accused of colluding with water demons. In the old days, village fortune-tellers who looked into the water to foretell events would first turn to Aspid.

Prince Aspid, like other demons, loves sacrifices. It is believed that a sudden increase in the drownings of people or cattle means that Prince Aspid is hungry for sacrifices. In the old days, people who sought Aspid's favor spilled the blood of black roosters into water or threw them in to drown. Sailors tried not to take women on board because they believed that Aspid would demand that they give the woman to him and would arrange a storm until they did. If a storm began, they threw the woman into the sea. Aspid usually takes only the souls of drowned people and throws the bodies ashore. If a body is not found, it means that the drowned man has become a clapper, a restless corpse that serves evil spirits. It is believed that people who are excellent swimmers from birth are born from the union of a woman and a water demon. Fishermen appeal to water demons by pouring tobacco, vodka, and honey into the water and even throwing in coins. Beekeepers especially revere water demons. According to legend, the first queen bee was given to people by Prince Aspid. This is why bees are considered very spiritual in many religions, including voodoo.

Aspid does not teach mages. Like many other demons, he can only give knowledge in exchange for an offering. Mages can form a contract with him about something and enter into an arrangement on mutually beneficial terms. Aspid often fights with the master of the forest, Prince Enarh, over his spheres of influence in the swampy waters of the forest. As a result, either a swamp swallows up a forest, or the forest claims the swamp.

Kupala Night,* the night of July 6,† is when the demon Aspid is

---

*Kupala Night, originally a pagan fertility and cleansing rite, is celebrated in Ukraine, Poland, Belarus, and Russia as a midsummer festival during which people sing and dance around bonfires.

†In the Julian calendar Kupala Night fell during the summer solstice, June 20 to 22. A note about dates: The entire Orthodox world used the Julian calendar, which is

reputed to have been born. According to popular belief, people should not bathe while drunk on this night because the water demon may drown them. This rule does not apply to mages. On the contrary, they are encouraged to bathe while drunk.

PRINCE ENOCH

The fifth in the pantheon is the demon of lust and debauchery, the great Prince Enoch. Like other fallen angels who took part in the riot, he was cast from heaven and became a demon. Enoch creates irrepressible lust and debauchery in people. He tears families apart by inciting couples to infidelity while arranging quarrels and turmoil in their families. He also pushes people to a passion for drinking and gambling. He is always cheerful and reckless at any time of the day and night but is most powerful at night. He tries to seduce as many people as possible into sinful deeds in the dark, sometimes driving them to insanity and death. He likes to patronize mages, to give them lesser demons as personal protectors for their dark deeds, as well as to fulfill the requests of sorcerers. He has the appearance of a man with a goat head, hooves, and a body covered with shaggy, black hair and has a huge, eternally erect member. Elizuda, the wife of the demon Enoch, also known as the Plague, was born from an inconsolable soul and became a demoness. She constantly strives to push God's people to lust and debauchery so that people become mired in sin and lose control of their souls to evil spirits.

(*cont.*) currently thirteen days behind our modern civil calendar, until March 1924. At that time, the bishops of the church in Greece unilaterally converted their dioceses to the new calendar, by deleting thirteen days at once, so that the religious calendar would coincide with the civil. This means that Orthodox Christians across the world were now celebrating the important celebrations of faith out of sync with each other, which impacted the unity of the Orthodox Church. The majority of the Orthodox in the world did not accept this change, as is still the case in places like Russia, Serbia, Jerusalem, and Georgia.

PRINCE ENARH

The sixth in the pantheon, great Prince Enarh, is the master of the forest. His assistants are all lesser forest demons. He owns all that is in the forest, its flora and fauna. All mages must turn to him before starting work in his territory. According to the Old Slavic tradition of demons, Enarh is commonly called the forest spirit. The demon Enarh, in his true appearance, looks like a half beast, half man of great size. He has a thick coat, horns, beard, and both hooves and claws. But he can appear in any guise, as any beast, bird, tree, or bush and even a mushroom. Many believe that it is not possible to see him at all because he does not have a true appearance. Instead he appears in the form of an unexpected wind or sound. His appearance is usually associated with various weather phenomena, such as whirlwinds or a sharp gust. He, like other demons, is surrounded by his closest assistants and an army of lesser demons. He provides mages with personal assistants. His assistants in the forest are driftwood, twisted trees, ravines, impassable thick thickets, forest crossings, and swamps.

The leader of the sixth principality of demons, Enarh often goes out into the forest thicket with his retinue. He visits the depths of Earth only when necessary to get advice from the higher princes. There is also a belief that Enarh stays in the depths of Earth, ascending only as necessary, and sends his assistants to work in the forests.

Enarh's assistants are the demon Haley, who is responsible for fields, and the demon Seneon, who poses a danger for anyone who goes into the forest. Like any other demon, he strives in every way to harm people, taking away their souls. He immediately starts messing with and mocking anyone who enters the forest. He tries to lead people off the path and into impassable thickets and swamps, making them wander, circling for hours, while predatory animals lie in wait. Enarh and his assistants will, however, protect mages in his service in every possible way. It is believed that those who are not mages but who simply seek favor with Enarh, by appealing to him with offerings, become successful hunters, mushroom pickers, herbalists, and shepherds. It is believed that the forest master favors mute and hunchback people, leading them to good places to gather mushrooms and berries. Because of this, such people are often accused of collusion with the forest spirit.

PRINCESS DEATH

The seventh place in the pantheon is occupied by the great Princess Death, the mistress of the cemeteries, who is in the seventh circle of hell. All the souls of the deceased are in her keeping while awaiting the Last Judgment of God. Hordes of cemetery demons serve her. They dwell at cemetery crossroads and are known for their inordinate power and cruelty. Mages call them the seventh demonic army. The great princess is strong and continually growing stronger due to the constant replenishment of cemeteries with the souls of dead people, who await to be chosen by either God or Satan, her uncle. All mages must address Princess Death before starting work in her domain. They have to request permission to bring any particular dead person or graveyard demon into their dark works, and mages regularly work in cemeteries.

In the distant past, even before the emergence of black magic as a defined system, the master of death was considered the dominant force over the world of the dead. He was the prototype of the great Princess Death. In ancient Russian pagan epics and legends, he was called Koshchy the Immortal. His name stems from the ancient word *kosh* or *kosht*, which means "ossification or death." He was immortal because death cannot die.

In times long past, there were no burials. The deceased were cremated, and their ashes spread on mounds. Over time, people developed theories about death and the afterlife. Someone ruled the demons of the world of the dead and the cemetery, but it wasn't believed to be the mistress of the cemeteries. Death was a force that dominated the world of the dead, not burial grounds. However, even now, in some remote provinces among some especially tribal mages, it is customary to call the force in the cemeteries the master of the cemetery. Although it cannot be proved, that isn't correct. It's possible that such errors and discrepancies arose from the echoes of various ancient Western religions and cults in which there were two equal powers dominating the world of the dead and one single force that combined the characteristics of both male and female. Also, many mages occasionally see the silhouette of a dark male figure in the cemetery during a ritual. They then begin to believe that it is the mysterious master of the cemetery. This is not the case, however, because no such master exists. It may be one of the seventh army demons who serve Death, the mistress of the cemeteries, such as the demon of grief or one of the lesser assistant demons.

According to legend, Death was the daughter of God and the wife of one of the most influential angels in God's council. He made mistakes, and God ordered him to be executed and sent him to hell. The wife of this angel, nicknamed the Black Widow, eternally grieved for her husband and harbored a fierce anger at God and tried to harm him. God starved her for her schemes, until she was a thin woman in black robes. She became so emaciated that she turned into a skeleton, and so hungry that no amount of souls could sate her. When the rebellion began in heaven, she did not hesitate to side with the rebels and was cast out. Satan, noticing her ever-yearning disposition after her husband's death and her own starvation, appointed her mistress of the cemeteries. She was given dominion over all human souls awaiting the Last Judgment of God. She could have her fill of souls and keep all unclean souls. She also had all the demons of the cemetery at her disposal. Many mages claim that she appears before them in the guise of a tall, stately woman in a hooded black dress that completely covers her, head to toe. But when the garment or hood flies open, they see that she is a skeleton with a bare skull for a face. Also, many claim that she has small horns on her head and wings at her back. Large tears fall from her empty eye sockets. There is an inverted cross drawn on the back of her cloak. She carries a sharp scythe with which she reaps human lives, first by taking their legs, then their hands, then their heads. Then she makes the dying people drink fire and forces their souls out of their bodies. Dying people claim to experience these feelings. Per their reports, Death may be invisible, a beauty, or a terrible old woman.

She is noiseless and often unexpected. Before her arrival, a person is usually visited by one of her assistant demons, the demon of grief (commonly known as Grief) and the demoness of disaster (commonly known as Disaster). He can fend Death off for a while if he knows that she will come soon. She can also be a dense fog of dark color. Although Death joined the rebels without hesitation, she believed that the rebels would never defeat God. Therefore she was not as severely punished by God and received a place of honor not only in the order of Satan but also in the grace of God himself. As the guardian of human souls awaiting the Last Judgment of God, it is believed that she holds a place between God and Satan. To this day, she goes to both God in heaven and Satan in the bowels of Earth for orders. She preserves a kind of neutrality between the two sides.

The demon of grief and the demoness of disaster are the brother and sister of Princess Death. Each of them has close assistants. Another important role is played by the Tyasovitsa demonesses, the twelve daughters of the demon Herod (they are commonly known as twisters, fevers, and hags). They arose from the union of Herod and Princess Death.

PRINCE INDIK

The eighth in the pantheon of demons of Russian black magic is the great black Prince Indik. After he was cast out of heaven with the other fallen angels and turned into a demon, he settled in the depths of Earth. The demon Indik ascends to the surface extremely rarely. When he does, he appears in the guise of a gigantic horned beast on four powerful paws, dragging a long, thick tail behind him. Indik causes earthquakes, natural disasters, and terrible destruction. He seeks to bring death, suffering, and unhappiness to all people and life-forms. In the old days, mages who wished to conjure earthquakes, natural disasters, and destruction appealed to him.

Indik dwells in the bowels of Earth and does not like to ascend to the surface unless people disturb him or a mage asks for his favor. He may receive orders from Satan to bring about destruction and earthquakes on this or that part of Earth.

PRINCE MAFAWA

The pantheon's ninth place is occupied by the great Prince Mafawa. Before he fell to Earth and was still an angel in heaven, he was part of the angelic council. After falling to Earth and becoming a demon, Mafawa settled in the bowels of Earth. Satan appointed him the keeper of all the treasures of Earth in recognition of his insatiability. Mafawa is the demon of avarice, envy, and profit. He prefers to be in the depths of Earth, protecting gold and other riches. He can bring earthquakes and destruction to whoever approaches his horde without permission. He periodically goes to Earth's surface to instill greed and a passion for profit in people, as well as to seduce people to Satan's side by offering them various blessings and riches. He also protects treasures. Sometimes people who dig for treasure appeal to him with a request to guard the treasures from anyone else or allow only those who have fulfilled certain conditions to reach them. People approach him with requests to make them rich and successful. He will be generous with them if they fulfill all his conditions. Like other demons, he can appear in any guise, transforming himself from his true image of a giant reptile with a huge belly, four thick legs, and a horned snake's head with a huge and terrible fire-breathing maw.

THE HOME OF DEMONS

The home of demons is located in Earth's depths. The rebel angels who fell after Satan, the first to be cast from heaven, landed in the vicinity of the present-day city of Jerusalem. God cast out the rebels to die but did not realize they might survive. The bowels of Earth are filled with fire, heat, poisonous gases, untold riches, huge underground lakes, rivers, and seas, but the demons cobbled together a home there. They chose huge underground spaces and erected a luxurious abode there for themselves.

The place where demons live is commonly known as hell, although in reality hell is directly in the Pit of Fire, and demons do not live in the pit because everything that enters that place will be destroyed. Demons actually live on the threshold of hell. As stated earlier, the home of demons has nine circles, with Satan in the first circle located near the center of Earth. The demon princes occupy every other circle, according to seniority, with the lowest placed closest to the surface. Prince Mafawa occupies the ninth, and last, circle, located near the surface of Earth.

Not all of the demons are constantly in their homes, however. They can move freely among all the circles of hell, and they may ascend to the surface for their daily business (principally gathering human souls). The princes themselves prefer to remain in their principalities and send their many assistants out to do their bidding. The souls of people who have done evil in their lives go straight to hell, or rather they unite with the evil spirits whom they nourish and become one with them.

Most of the souls of the dead are placed at the disposal of Princess Death. The souls of people who lead righteous lives go straight to heaven, where they nourish God, who absorbs them into him. The others go to the Pit of Fire, and if the evil spirits in Death's kingdom number enough, she could swallow up the heavenly throne. The demons of the first, second, and third circle of hell feed upon the souls of blasphemers and apostates, murderers and tormentors, suicides who died in battles, and mages. The demons of the fourth circle of hell feed upon the souls of those who perished in water and suicides who killed themselves by drowning; the fifth circle upon the souls of great lechers and philanderers, hedonists, pimps, seducers, drunkards, gluttons, idlers, pedophiles, and rapists; the sixth circle upon the souls of those who die in the woods and are torn apart by wild beasts; the seventh circle is full of souls awaiting the Last Judgement, as previously mentioned; the eighth circle feeds upon the souls of those killed in earthquakes, fires, severe frosts, and hurricanes; and the ninth circle feeds upon the souls of the cruel, the rich, the spendthrifts, the swindlers, the materialistic soul sellers, and the deceivers. There are some other similar theories adopted in the tradition of black magic, but this is the most popular one.

4

THE THREE FORCES, THE SOUL, AND SATANISM

According to the teachings of mages, there are three main forces: the first is God, the Heavenly Father, with his saints and angels; the second is Satan, with his demonic army; and the third is Death, who controls ghosts or spirits and graveyard demons.

God is the all-knowing who absorbs all other minds (people's souls) and therefore encompasses saints and angels. They are attached to him and do not have their own free will. Mages believe that God is a noncorporeal being of highly intelligent energy. God is great because he created cosmic expanses, and man could not exist without it. Despite all this, he is not a source of good, as the clergy say.

Contrary to his depiction in most mainstream religions, God is by no means eternal or omnipresent. His abode is heaven (immaterial reality), which should be separated from the first and second "heavens"; that is, from the atmosphere and outer space. Even according to the saints, there are many "evil spirits" in the air. In medieval grimoires they called demons spirits who inhabited the air. According to legend, the devil cannot rise above the moon.

The second force in the universe is the devil. The word *devil* is Greek and was brought into Russian less than a thousand years ago. However, ancient Slavs knew that there were dark gods and spirits deep in Earth. The devil is the name of all the evil forces as a whole. Just like God, it includes many souls that Satan has absorbed, as well as the entire black army of the demonic regiments, led by Satan himself. The third force, Death, or the mistress of the cemeteries, is referred to as an Unclean Force and is part of the pantheon of Russian evil.

THE ORIGIN OF THE WORLD

God arose as a spark in darkness. He gave rise to other minds, separating them from himself. To remain conscious, he needs to consume the same kind of energy of which he consists. To achieve this, he separated particles from himself and created assistants made of the same nonmaterial. These angels (the eldest son being Satanel, who originally was nicknamed the Prince of Peace) were the first of his creations but not the last. Together they created the universe, the sun and Earth, planets and their satellites, and the lifeless cosmos. But at the end God was tired and decided to replenish his strength. He created man on one of the planets, as well as diverse flora and fauna, and used them to maintain his existence. Some of the angels who had helped him, after being cast out of heaven, settled into the created kingdoms: in the forest, in the waters, and so on. And so, God created the world.

THE ORIGIN OF MAN

Black magic tells us directly that God created man not just as an entity unto himself or as an image of God but for his own personal needs, as a means to reproduce souls. He thinks of and treats humans the same way we think of laboratory monkeys or beef cattle—the former used for medical experiments and the latter slaughtered without remorse. That is the "love" he feels for us. Islam, Buddhism, and Hinduism have tried each in their own way to comprehend the entity that takes righteous souls and to understand why these souls do not return.

The Heavenly Father endowed Adam with a particle of his essence, a tiny fraction of his nonmaterial intelligent energy, and also created a helpmate for him, Eve. God needed them to reproduce obedient progeny. The subsequent brood on Earth was intelligent (i.e., endowed with souls). The rest of the flora and fauna lacked that spark to become self-conscious and act on their own behalf. God then took back all of the multiplied energy of people at their deaths.

Paradise was an incubator of new souls, of new food for the starving god. It ceased to exist when the Heavenly Father lost control of soul reproduction. As mentioned earlier, even before the war in heaven, Aspid, in the guise of a snake, appeared to Eve and revealed to her the truth about why she and Adam were created. This is connected to a story in the Bible (Gen. 3:8) in which God walked around Eden, looking for Adam and Eve, who hid from him among the trees.

After Aspid taught Eve to receive pleasure from intimacy, she taught Adam, and they began to sleep with each other for pleasure—something that God hated. He called it the sin of fornication, as it deprived him of control over souls and their reproduction. Souls created in lust are tainted goods, and God will not accept them. Afterward people were banished from paradise. Those who fell from God's grace were visited by his brothers and sons (demons) and gave birth to their offspring. He decided to sweep them from the face of Earth with the heavenly flood. God deprived man of grace. He created illnesses, depriving them of longevity. As you know, Adam and his descendants have been cursed for hundreds of years. The threshold age was set at 120 years, and few people in human memory have exceeded this age. Women began to experience agony when giving birth to children, and from then on people had difficulty feeding themselves. God commanded all this in anger at the fact that the souls were mired in passions and he could no longer take them.

According to one of the legends, when the daughter of Adam became the first person to die, and he and Eve were grieving, Satan came to visit them in the guise of a kind old man. He told them he would revive the daughter if Adam signed a contract in blood on his daughter's skull, rendering all dead souls to Satan. He wanted all the souls of Adam's descendants to come to him. The devil would have quickly gained incredible power. He planned to use this power to overthrow his father from the heavenly throne and rule over heaven himself. But that did not happen. God sent one of his sons to Earth, an angel in the form of a man, Jesus Christ, who descended to hell and broke Satan's contract with man. God then sent angels in the guise of mortals to Earth to establish his church and the mass gathering of souls in favor of the Heavenly Father. Jesus Christ was also sent to Earth to establish God's church on Earth and to lead people through the rite of baptism. This hallowed ritual is in fact a sale of the soul to God and even greatly resembles the act of offering a soul to the devil.*

And so, for the past two thousand years, the soul of a newborn does not belong to anyone. The rights to it can be transferred at will, either by laying it down to God (through the rite of baptism and calling the child a servant of the Lord) or by selling the child's soul to the devil in return for earthly benefits. This is not the best way, however, because it is much more reasonable not to bargain with the devil but to serve his cause instead. Then he will not absorb you when you die but rather keep you in his kingdom as a half demon. He will prolong the existence of a heretic for all eternity. One of the biggest misconceptions (or rather, conscious deceptions) of mainstream religions is that the soul belongs to God from birth. This is not the case. (Incidentally, this concept of human origin does not contradict Darwin's theory, because scientists

---

*In an Orthodox Christian baptism, the priest cuts three locks of the child's hair, rolls the hair in wax, and tosses the wax ball into the baptismal font while reading spells or praying. Then the priest dips the child into the font and renounces Satan. As a final act, the priest and the parents spit on the floor to the west, toward Satan, and bind the child to God as his subject and his future meal.

have not yet answered the question of why some primates developed and became *Homo sapiens* while others remained apes.)

FATE AND PREDESTINATION

Of course there is no real freedom in the broad sense of the word. We all die sooner or later, and therefore at least some of us will fall into the realm of Death, the seventh circle of hell. The rest will be absorbed by the forces or attached to them, either to God or his irrepressible son, Satan. We are not free to choose our parents (though I'm sure the Hindus would disagree) or our place of birth. Of the few of us who are sent back to Earth to attract new souls to the devil, we are not given the right to choose to be reborn or the place and time of our rebirth.

Mages recognize the power of occult rites and the possibility of changing the natural course of events. However, it is known that even a death curse does not guarantee a person's rapid death, because there are healers. Sometimes God does not allow a particular person to be removed from Earth if he needs him for something else. For example, saints and apostles are suppliers of new souls for the Heavenly Father, and no mage, however powerful, can oppose the very king of heaven, the origin of all power.

WHAT IS THE SOUL AND
WHAT IS IT TO THE DEVIL AND GOD?

As noted earlier, God created everything on Earth (plants and animals) for the cultivation of people or, more precisely, souls, as food for himself and his assistants, the angelic army—just we humans absorb the same kind of organic matter from which we're made: fats, proteins, and carbohydrates. Everyone and everything needs energy to exist. When a man and a woman mate, a new life is created, and at the same time a new soul is formed. People's lives were initially unlimited, but God made the decision to end their lives when he needed energy. He ordered his angels to make it so. He planned everything and kept it under his complete control.

The Heavenly Father planted a lot of white-light teachings on Earth that suggested that the real world is vain and insignificant and your entire life should be a preparation for death. Mainstream religions teach that behind the cover of the grave, your suffering will end, and you will be surrounded by angels with harps. Divine music and peace will emanate from them. If you are a man, beautiful houris (young female virgins) will attend you, and wine will flow like a river. You may even reach nirvana, and earthly privations will cease. Needless to say, such religions have always been readily supported by the ruling class: endure your masters here, work for a pittance, and God will reward you in death after taking you to heaven.

Satanel, one of the strongest angels, decided to rebel and take the place of his father-creator. To this end, he swayed a third of the angelic army to his side and arranged a trick. He took the process of cultivation of souls out of God's control, and he corrupted people by introducing them to lust. Satanael became the demon Satan after the rebellion failed and he was cast out. God threw him and all the rebels into the very core of Earth, to destroy them in the Pit of Fire. The Pit of Fire itself was originally created to destroy "defective" souls and straying angels. As a result of all this upheaval, the process of cultivating souls became uncontrollable and underwent many changes. From then on, people had to take better care of themselves without the help of God's mercy. The life span of people has become limited due to many factors, and people's souls are no longer directly given over to God's keeping (commonly known as heaven) but fall to Death, as a member of the angelic council. She joined the rebels and as a result turned into a demon. She consumes human souls just as God, the angels, and other demons do, but she is relatively neutral and for the time being is the mistress of all souls.

Only the souls of righteous people who have been trying to give their soul to him all their lives go straight to God. The souls that Satan manages to collect and seduce in some way during their lives go to the devil's home (known as hell) along with the souls of the greatest sinners, because God disdains them. For the time being, God is not trying to completely destroy his rebellious son and his army. They are not a small force. He only threatens them with the Last Judgment, when he will descend to Earth along with Death and arrange a trial of souls. He may then gain immense power and, full of unmerciful force, finally destroy the Unclean Force of the demons and all the sinful souls he does not need. Satan, in turn, feels that God has greater power and does not dare to try again. He only gathers the power of souls made up of the same inexplicable substance from which he, God, and the angels were made. He needs mages (after all, the souls of all people associated with sorcery are food for the Unclean One).

Death, as a neutral force, holds this growing energy. In fact, the Last Judgment may come when God loses access to the nourishment that souls provide and, starving, arranges a trial. The devil (in general, all demonic warriors are called the devil or the Unclean Force among mages) will swallow it up or destroy God because the majority of souls will be in his keeping. This struggle has gone on for untold ages and will continue for untold ages, with God and Satan both periodically sending great preachers and villains among the humans to improve their position. Both may be launching new projects and studies into the production of that most incomprehensible substance, the soul. People occasionally observe this in the form of all kinds of incomprehensible phenomena. In addition, it is believed that people as we know them are not the first creation for the cultivation of souls. There are also slightly different theories of this worldview accepted in the tradition of black magic. One is that the devil was the original creator, and God is his creation. In this theory, he is a very cunning god and collects souls with his ubiquitous, sly propaganda through churches and priests. Another theory suggests that God and the devil are two originally opposing energies that created man by giving him a soul but who cannot share the fruits of their labor.

These are only theories.

RUSSIAN BLACK MAGIC, PAGANISM, AND MODERN SATANISM

Russian black magic is a religious system based on a foundation of heretic ideas, a specific pantheon of Satan and demons, and—as we will see later in the book—well-defined spellwork and collaboration with demons. Though Russian black magic shares some features and common background with modern Satanism, they are not the same. In fact, there seem to be more commonalities between paganism in general (as a worldview, which often includes both "light" and "dark" gods) and modern Satanism, rather than with Russian black magic specifically and modern Satanism. In this section I discuss the similarities between paganism and Satanism.

Satanism does not always stem from Christianity. The worship of the dark gods has always existed and is widespread. At the same time, the dark gods are not necessarily evil but are, as a rule, the gods of the lower world. They follow the structure and laws of that world. There are also the gods of retribution who are sometimes opposed to the unscrupulous light, which is striving to make everyone "bright" and "good." Dark gods maintain equilibrium in the universe; they are one side of this balance. Without them no society or order can exist.

Satan in the medieval tradition is not so much a character in Christian mythology as an expression of the dark gods necessary for the existence of any society and any person. The functions of the dark gods eventually fell to Satan. Unfortunately, in modern (and in past) Europe and America, Satan is seen as a notorious evil. However, if you seriously delve into his functions, what he does, what he actually wants, and why, then it becomes clear that the universe simply could not exist without him. The actions of Satan and the rebellious angels against God led to the formation of a soul and free will. They ceased to be puppets; moreover, in Slavic paganism a person is not someone's puppet. Neither gods nor other people are beholden to anyone, and this is directly related to Satan's revolt against God.

In modern society, those claiming to be pagans, who only want to play at paganism in part because they like the image it gives them, tend to pay close attention to society. The authentic pagan does not care what others think of him. His inherent free will allows him to take any position with inner conviction. If he believes that his worldview is right, and his actions are necessary, he is entitled to think and act as he sees fit. Unlike believers in monotheistic religions, he is not rigidly tied to the rules of God and society.

Sacred paganism, like Satanism, is not connected to people but relies on the laws of the universe. Let's give an analogy: World constants, say, a number or a gravitational constant, exist independently of people. Paganism, much like Satanism, is based on the will of the dark gods and not on a person's opinion about what is at present convenient or suitable for him. Both worldviews rely on studying objective laws and not slipping into vague, debilitating statements such as "God works in mysterious ways."

In Satanism there is a concept of man's departure from the norms of social life but also from humanity in general. From the point of view of Satanism, mankind must be destroyed and something worthy put in its place. In a similar way, dark paganism sees present-day humans as harmful: they are a mold that rots Earth and will even destroy the cosmos. The positions of paganism and Satanism coincide here. Paganism, however, is not about the physical destruction of each person but rather about the need for a new type of human to emerge that is fundamentally different from current humans. However, this does not mean that this new human is the same, only slightly stronger and smarter.

Christianity asks the wretched to "pray and be saved" so that they may enter the kingdom of heaven. In paganism the wretched are not asked to worship; instead, individuals must grow, develop, and become something more. Satanism expects the same. Of course the methodologies and approaches of paganism and Satanism differ. Often pagans are criticized for having an overvalued desire to win the masses. But their drive to interact with others is grounded in their deisre to help people to break away from the status quo. If more people do not break away from the masses, then the same mold will continue to grow, rotting the world.

If you look at the essence of their worldviews, Satanism and paganism have much more in common than not. Their differences are mostly related to practical social issues.

Another important thing that unites paganism and Satanism is the refusal to worship, but instead to *honor*. Worship contradicts the essence of Satanism. Satan, if we trace the mythology, refused to worship or be worshipped, even if that meant he had no chance of victory when God declared himself omnipotent. (As we have seen, some aspects of the archetypal image that modern Satanism has of Satan were influenced by Christianity, such as the legend of Satan's pride and rebellion, which does not originate with the pagans because they do not have a concept of a singular god.)

If you think about it, to worship someone is to insult him; it is better to honor him. Pagans honor their gods. Gods can be praised for their help (or for no particular reason) or, conversely, for not causing harm. For a pagan, the gods are not some abstract absolute but partners, even if they are more powerful than the people themselves. Pagan gods, though more perfect than humans, are still imperfect. This makes them more real than any monotheistic symbol.

However, in the Judeo-Christian tradition, God is not perfect. At times, Yahweh in the Old Testament behaves in a most human way: spiteful, unjust, and unbalanced. Maybe because in Judaism he is all alone as a god: he has no friends or brothers. The essential difference here is only that pagans always perceive their gods as real people.

Pagans are much more inclined to a personal perception of the gods than Satanists. However, whether there is a personal or impersonal perception makes no difference. The main thing is not to forget that this is only a model and not the absolute truth.

Satan has many faces. According to American occultist Anton Szandor LaVey, for example, Lucifer personifies knowledge, while Belial, the Hebrew name for the devil, personifies independence. You can draw a parallel with the pagans who have, if I may say so, a separate god, in principle, for every situation. Pagans turn, depending on the situation, to different gods; Satanists turn to various aspects of Satan. Pagans have historically formed a pantheon. Satanists have a more abstract perception and do not need a name to refer to a certain aspect of being.

Moreover, for pagans, the mythological confrontation between Odin and Loki does not mean invoking only one of them and never another. Satanists act similarly. They appeal to one of Satan's names, personifying the aspect required at the moment. This aspect of Satanism may pose a stumbling block to pagans, as it is difficult for them to understand that Satanism is not monotheism and, in fact, not theism at all.

The rituals and ceremonies that pagans perform are quite pleasant for their participants. There is music, dancing, alcoholic beverages, and interaction with the opposite sex. Who wouldn't like this kind of a religious festival? You are not fasting or abstaining from anything; you are not kneeling for long periods of time or beating your forehead on the floor. And communication with the gods is a personal matter for everyone. Moreover, the priest cannot provide much help in this (compare with Christianity: "Outside the church there is no salvation"). The pagan priest is not an interpreter of divine revelations. He can recite one of the myths (his direct duty) by heart, but he will not impose his opinion on anyone and present it as the absolute truth.

Remember the Greek oracles. They said very vague things and never interpreted the meanings themselves. For another significant commonality: both Satanists and pagans respect the right of others to their interpretation of the image of Satan or God. There are no dogmas of faith, commandments, or restrictions. The satanic commandments of LaVey, who established LaVeyan Satanism in 1966, are just recommendations, and Satanism itself existed long before the publication of *The Satanic Bible* in 1969 by LaVey. Furthermore, this bible is not at all a holy book. As there can be no dogmas by definition for a Satanist, how, then, can there be a collection of absolute truths? *The Satanic Bible* is very good publicity with a lot of clever ideas, including between the lines and not only on the surface. However, it was written with a completely unambiguous goal: to encourage people to join the Church of Satan, which LaVey organized. It is a very good book, if commercial, but not holy. No one demands that Satanists live only as described in LaVey's bible. Moreover, I do not agree with some of the thoughts expressed by LaVey—for instance, that modern Satanism is a religion. I believe that Satanism is a worldview.

In *The Satanic Bible,* LaVey cites the formula: religion equals dogma plus ceremony. What is interesting is that nowhere in *The Satanic Bible* or his other books does he describe any dogma. I think that he claimed Satanism to be a religion specifically to avoid frightening away potential adherents who are accustomed to external restrictions. As for the ceremony, he describes magical rituals. Still, he writes that improvisation is the determining factor for a mage and not the careful pronunciation of the true names of Satan and other hackneyed phrases such as *sapienti sat.** Those who do not know how to delve into the meaning between the lines and who need to thoroughly ponder everything are not needed in Satanism. So it is very likely that LaVey is trying to filter out those who are unable to think independently. By the

---

*Latin phrase meaning that something can be understood without any explanation as long as the listener has wisdom and common sense.

way, the word *bible* derives from the Greek word *biblion,* which means, simply, "book," so the accusation that LaVey borrowed the title from Christianity is similar to the observation that he borrowed the format from the Christian Bible instead of creating an original book with no similarity to the former.

Pagans not only recognize the existence of all the gods of other pantheons but respect their power as well. Pagans faced the issue of religious wars only with the spread of Christianity and only against Christian "baptizers." Remember that paganism has existed much longer than any monotheist religion. Imagine, then, that among the many gods a new one appears demanding exclusive power. Think of it this way: you have your social circle (your gods and those of your friends), and then a stranger (the Christian church) approaches, uninvited, and announces that he is taking over and replacing your gods with his one God—and simply tells your gods to go away.

On the topic of reverence, Satanists and pagans honor different objects. Pagans honor not just the gods but also pay homage to ancestors, to the clan, and to the tribe. These are impersonal; that is, the ancestors are not honored personally but simply as those who continued the race of which pagans are a part. Paganism is inconceivable without national (or tribal) traditions. The interests of the clan stand above all. This does not, however, apply to all pagan sects but is true for Russian paganism. Among the Scandinavians, the connection with ancestors and relatives was in the fabric of the social sphere and completely outside the framework of religion. It says that Valhalla takes brave, not aristocratic, warriors. In this case, personal qualities are more important than origin. Vikings took soldiers into their squads regardless of pedigree, and admission to the squad was a very important act. The patronage of Odin was automatically extended to each volunteer. By the way, many Scandinavian heroes typically did not know who their fathers were—a situation that is absolutely inconceivable among the Slavs, who are very attached to their ancestors and honor them before any other gods or spirits.

For Satanists something otherworldly can pose a bit of a challenge, but for a pagan such a concept is generally absurd. If it does not work to interact with one god, he can turn to another. For Christians, turning to another god is inconceivable and frightening: they cannot offend the sole God they depend on! In paganism, there are no prescribed fasts or abstinences from anything, such as from meat and alcohol. If you want or need something, no one will forbid it or stop you. Why is it, one might wonder, that the monotheistic God forbids certain foods and behaviors but the pagans do not? In Satanism it is even simpler: there is no god to forbid anything to anyone.

These two worldviews also do not proselytize. Has anyone ever heard of a pagan or Satanist missionary? Both worldviews are cheerful. They want to take what they think is necessary from life. Simply put, if an afterworld exists, then when we get there, we will play by those rules. Meanwhile, since the afterworld remains unknown to everyone, there is nothing to worry about. Most important, Satanism and paganism are *not* religions in the literal sense of the word. Religion necessarily involves worshipping someone. In this case the more correct term is *worldview*. Again, paganism and Satanism are both philosophies of action, not passivity. They will not turn the other cheek when struck; instead, "whoever comes to us with a sword will come and perish by the sword." Although everyone regards charity as a virtue, it is sometimes engendered by vanity, laziness, or fear and often all three. This is where the difference lies. In paganism, the worship of dark gods is not forbidden, but somehow not accepted—in the common version, at least. But given that the pagan gods do not claim to be absolute good or evil, the difference is not so significant. In addition, the spheres of influence of the dark gods are far from everyday life, and not everyone is required to honor them (paganism adopts a horizontal structure, in contrast to vertical monotheism). However, if this happens, then neither other gods nor co-religionists will punish them. Pagans are not afraid and do not expect any god to climb, so to speak, into the sphere of influence of another, as no normal person will climb into another's soul and find out why he made an offering to Ares or, in the case of black mages, to Satan or his demons.

Both worldviews also have a sense of humor. If Satan is evil, pagans simply need to remember Loki, the mischievous shapeshifting Norse trickster god. Many religions have one or more trickster gods, like Loki in the old Norse religion, and Enki, the god of mischief and freshwater, in the Sumerian religion.

However, trickery should not be seen as necessarily evil. For instance, in the earliest known flood legend, one human, Uta-napishtim, is saved by Enki's trickery from the deluge sent by Enlil. Enlil had attempted numerous times to eradicate mankind because the noise from the cities where humans gathered was so great that Enlil couldn't sleep. Having been repeatedly foiled by Enki, Enlil had him swear not to reveal the coming deluge to any humans. Enki circumvents this by disclosing the sensitive information, not to Uta-napishtim himself, but to the hut in which he happens to live.

The point so far is that Christianity has inherited many traits from previous religions, and trickery is no exception. The trickster aspects of Satan have basis in both scripture and history. In scripture, you have situations such as the temptation of Eve, or Satan's attempts at twisting the gospel when Jesus is fasting.

When did Christ, Yahweh, Allah, or even Buddha smile or joke? Why is this so? (I will not specifically delve into this aspect; you can consider it for yourself.) In addition, it should be noted that pagans do not perceive allegories literally. Vikings, the best navigators of their time, knew geography well, I'm sure, and hardly any of them represented the world in the form of a giant ash tree. Sailing on the sea and thinking that you are sitting on a tree is a bit strange. It's the same with the myths of creation. They do not need to be taken literally; they carry a much deeper meaning—for example, Odin ritualistically sacrificing himself to find the runes.

Pagans and Satanists are pragmatists, although pagans are much more so. Pagans believe that our world is created and populated by the children of the creator (gods) and grandchildren (people). Satanists, as a rule, deny both the very fact of creation and, in particular, that God sits and looks after the world created by him: Is there nothing else for him to do? However, these differing beliefs do not result in actual differences in behavior. Pagans (let us take Russians as an example) consider themselves to be the children of the family. Their goal is the continuation of the act of creation and the improvement of people to the level of the gods. Although it should be noted here that for most pagan sects the idea that life should be lived adequately is more typical. Slavic paganism is largely atypical because of the fragmented nature of Slavic tribes and their lack of a clear social organization. However, they do aspire to live with dignity a priori and are engaged in self-improvement. Satanists aspire to self-perfection for purely selfish reasons. But again, the result is the same: no one stands still, claiming to be the "crown of creation," and ceases to strive and evolve. Neither worldview operates with the concepts of absolute good and evil: these concepts are strictly for the individual to interpret. Both also espouse taking responsibility for your actions. Just like a Satanist, a pagan will not blame the devil for bad behavior or a bad outcome and claim innocence. You decide how to act and have only yourself to blame for your actions. This characteristic of Satanists and pagans is similar to rationalism.

Neither paganism nor Satanism recognize an ultimate goal of existence, such as to die and go to heaven. Rather, they see a path, a way of living, versus striving toward a specific goal. Life is a ray that tends in a direction and not necessarily a straight line—the geometry of existence is not Euclidean. After all, if you achieve your goal, what is there left to do? Both practices also believe that no concept of universal equality, as in Christianity, exists. The value of a person is not a given at birth but is earned through living. Each has his or her own criteria, but no pagan or Satanist will automatically respect someone. Everyone strives to deserve respect.

Equally important is that both worldviews place justice above charity: justice as it is understood in the secular world rather than some "higher" one. A characteristic error on the part of people who do not recognize this is the fear that lawlessness will happen if we remove the restrictions given by mainstream religions. For instance, they believe that everyone will immediately begin to kill and rape. As is known to any psychologist, the phrase "that's how everyone is" really means "that's how I am," but the person who says this is often unaware that he is talking about himself. The subconscious mind often deceives the conscious mind, and making such generalized statements is a sure sign that this does not apply to him but only to everyone else. Those who regulate rather than restrain their desires will not kill anyone (and if they need to, they will kill without breaking laws), but they will live the same way as before.

Equality, as proclaimed by monotheists, means that everyone is equal before the one God, and he rules them all. But by conforming to some faceless standard, people lose their individuality and become part of a faceless crowd. There is no reason. The emotions that arise are intensified by their communal nature. They are equal among equals, a status inspired by the ideas of the first among equals, who committed bloody massacres in the name of universal equality.

In childhood a child does not develop an individual identity (as it would be if the values of society were pagan or satanic) but rather a sense of belonging. From national organizations, such as the Boy Scouts, to reading circles at school and sports teams, everywhere in the subconscious mind it is introduced that "we" are more important than "I." And the "we" is very rarely determined by the individual's own choice. Does the child have any say in where he goes to school? If, however, he possesses a talent, he acts for the honor of the school. Eventually the individual is no longer able to act alone; he must belong to something.

He is afraid to be alone with his inner emptiness. He needs a crowd of like-minded people or at least a crowd united by an external slogan to be sure that he is not the only one.

Because pagans value autonomy, pagan priests fill a different role from that of Christian priests. Pagans in general and the priest in particular cannot answer for others before the gods. An interesting fact is that none of the pagan religions were aware of the concept of confession (naturally, in Satanism, confession is an even more absurd concept), whereas in Christianity, the notorious secret confession gave Christian priests great power over secular rulers. Both Satanists and pagans use private altars; neither need to go to a church, along with many others, to communicate with God or do magical work at an altar. The rituals are almost entirely individual, not public, and they do not require official priests. Although it should be noted that pagans do go to temples as a group during holidays, it is not because they are obliged to do this. They do not behave like Christians who feel obligated to attend church at Christmas and Easter. Pagan celebrations are like parties with a light religious touch. (However, in contrast to other paganisms, many Russian black magic spells are performed at church, as you will see in chapters 8 and 9.)

None of the pagan sects have prophets followed by crowds of people blinded by fanaticism, whereas the Judeo-Christian tradition abounds with such examples.

I think I have given enough examples to show that, despite the different initial assumptions and somewhat different ultimate goals, in everyday practice, all pagans, including Russian pagans, and Satanists have much in common. And, most importantly, their territories are not antagonistic to each other, and there is no confrontation in principle. However, it would be incorrect to end the conversation here. Satanism and Russian black magic have one advantage: you need self-confidence to call yourself a Satanist or black mage—if it's serious and not just teenage rebellion (which is very noticeable to committed Satanists).

Declaring yourself a pagan does not usually invite an extreme negative reaction from the majority of people.

I would like to point out another important common feature: neither worldview can be forcibly distributed. The person must voluntarily choose to be a part of them. Of course these are really worldviews, not meetings with rituals. From this, by the way, follows that, at least at the present stage, neither paganism nor Satanism can become the prevailing worldview. First, to follow them, you have to think on your own, and after two thousand years of learning to obey, people have simply forgotten how. Second, it is impossible because the modern state system can function normally only by constraining the populace's individuality to a general level to prevent a coup d'état.

So all those who are worried about the evil Satanists and cruel pagans who only think about how to sacrifice, all true believers can sleep peacefully. However, some experts in history may argue that paganism was also not always so liberal and respectful of other opinions. For example, Socrates's official accusation reads: "Socrates is accused of not recognizing the gods that the city recognizes and introducing other, new gods. He is accused of corrupting the youth. The required punishment is death." The phrase *new gods* referred to the famous demon of Socrates—his inner voice. The corruption of young people consisted of assembling them around him and posing riddles and tricky questions to them, teaching them how to think. If you are interested in the details, I would direct you to Plato's "Apology of Socrates."

The problem is that in ancient times society was considered superior to the individual. The person was perceived primarily as part of the clan, tribe, or city. But this ideology was not repressive, imposed from above: it was in people's blood. Everyone accepted such customs as something that was a part of them and did not aspire to anything else. And then came the notion of the individual. It emerged around the fifth and sixth centuries BCE, simultaneously in different countries. Thus, many religious and philosophical schools appeared in India, the most famous of which is Buddhism. They all taught that the meaning of religion is not in rituals that are mandatory for everyone but instead in personal self-improvement. (Compare this to the rigid caste system and required rituals in India.)

In Greece, philosophy appeared. This involved only a few, outstanding people, and society viewed them at best as crazy and at worst as dangerous rebels. Then the individuals began to gain power. At the same time, the authorities began to understand that religion could be a means of controlling the ordinary population.

However, beware that there were periods in the past when paganism began to turn into a kind of monotheism. Let us recall the worship of the emperor as a god in Roman times, with the order to put a statue in each temple.

Today's pagans, though very respectful of history, do not wish to restore that earlier paganism (which is impossible in most cases, as Christians have tried to destroy all pre-Christian gods and relics). There is no need to restore original paganism, which does not fit the mentality of modern man, and this approach is fully consistent with the antidogmatic nature of paganism (as well as Satanism). If you stupidly maintain the same doctrine or structure from one century to the next, you will become immersed in moldy dogmas, as in Christianity. The pagan worldview is active and continues to develop. Do not waste time reinventing the wheel.

The philosophy behind Paganism and Satanism worldviews is similar. It includes positive freedom and creativity and relies on the experiences of all previous generations (both positive and negative during the triumph of Christianity). In addition, Satanism uses the rich legacy of paganism, and pagans use modern philosophical ideas, including Satanism. What distinguishes these worldviews are not their external manifestations but the absence of dogma to determine behavior.

BLACK MAGIC
SPELLWORK

5

BASIC RULES AND
PRINCIPLES OF MAGIC

Over the centuries of its existence, black magic has developed its own academics. Like any human activity, practical black magic is based on certain postulates or principles. In addition to studying rituals, rites, and spells, every decent mage should learn these basic rules.

Many do not like to pay attention to the latest theories. To these people they seem boring and uninteresting. This is fundamentally the wrong position. Without theoretical knowledge, without constant internal work, all acquired skills will be stillborn. Most of us have cookbooks at home, but only people who regularly work at cooking can be called true cooks. Some people who decide to take the path of obtaining magical knowledge think of it as a kind of game. It may enthrall and excite them, but such people will never become real mages. These people are unable to be self-organized and disciplined, to develop the ability to concentrate, and to give up everyday pleasures.

Just as the scientific method entails a set of mandatory steps, practical magic also requires basic steps. In addition to general and special recommendations for the proper organization and conduct of certain magical rites, magical practices observe four basic rules, which are like four walls or four cornerstones. In a metaphysical sense, these rules form a magical pyramid. Considered separately, these rules do not seem very magical, but they create the necessary magical effect.

RULE NUMBER 1:
IMAGINATION

Practitioners must possess a strong imagination. A strong imagination is necessary for all creative personalities: writers, artists, designers, engineers. Without this it is impossible to create anything worthwhile. Within this rule is a subrule: the stronger your emotions are during your own fantasies, the stronger your chances of success. How you manifest these emotions is a purely personal matter. You may need to writhe on the ground and grind your teeth while vehemently hating someone or something. Various methods can help you elevate your emotions, such as vivid memories, sounds, smells, lights, and even dancing. Ease into the role gradually, spurring on your emotions through these sensory memories. The main thing is that it happens as intensely as possible. In the process of magical practices, you can use mental identification as well as identify some of your own deeply personal symbols.

Of course all this is difficult to achieve without creating a special place to perform the magic. The best places are those where no one will prevent the mage from carrying out her plan. Ideally the mage should have her own study, surrounded by all sorts of necessary things—statues, paintings, even trinkets. It is not always important that each of these things be genuine. For example, a high-quality reproduction of a well-known picture can still elicit a strong feeling and awaken fantasies. The main thing is that in this room you should feel comfortable and at home so that you would like to return there no matter what.

RULE NUMBER 2: WILL

A truly powerful black magic cannot exist without a strong, fiery will, which can be self-centered. Examples of willful self-centeredness are children and pampered adolescents who strongly resist even modest attempts to control their behavior. The mage uses her will like a lens to focus her most burning and strong emotions. The will must be constantly honed and sharpened like a battle sword.

To promote better concentration, meditation techniques borrowed from other practices can be helpful. Self-hypnosis is also necessary. The mage must learn to concentrate on what seems, at first glance, unimportant and seemingly unrelated things. Regularly practicing meditation and concentration will help you to connect to your magical will and provide a lasting and enduring effect. In general, such esotericism is very tiring for an ordinary person, but a mage is not an ordinary person.

Do not try to become vice regent of God on Earth; this will do nothing good for you. It is not brute force but perseverance that produces the greatest effect. That's why it's so important, at the beginning, not to try to do everything at once but instead to focus on achieving small things. Daily small victories are much more significant than one big triumph. These constant victories spur interest, first of all, toward oneself. Everything in its time.

You have to clearly understand what you want to get in a given period of time. During such sessions of magical auto-training, the key to success is always an unconditional and, if you like, uncompromising belief in yourself. That's why many spells end with the phrase "Let it be so!" This is a universal formula, an esoteric point, meaning that one or the other sentence is written just like that, but nothing else, and will not be changed. This is the code of the program, which forces it to work by a given specific algorithm. Regardless of whether it's black or white magic—or maybe red or blue—it sends a message that triggers a chain reaction that is always the same. So be it, it's only so and not otherwise. This is my will! I so desire, and I so decided! Period!

RULE NUMBER 3: FAITH

The third rule directly correlates with the second. The mage needs faith or, rather, unshakable faith. In general, faith does not recognize labels. The righteous can have it and the sinner can have it. Christians do not have a corner on faith. It is through faith that belief in ourselves is strengthened; the main enemy of faith is doubt. If you have no faith in your own strengths and capabilities, then all your endeavors are already doomed to failure.

Faith is a giant that carries your will on its mighty shoulders. And the will in this case can be represented metaphorically in the form of a furnace into which the molten metal of your imagination pours. That's how everything is interconnected. Do not be afraid of attacks of temporary megalomania. Without this, witchcraft is impossible. Absolute confidence in the correctness of your actions can work miracles. Without it, we would not have succeeded either in unconventional practices or in ordinary domestic activities.

Faith is closely related to another important concept; namely, the word of the mage. It is inadmissible for the mage to promise to perform or do something while even 1 percent of doubt about the possibility of accomplishing it remains in his mind. Violating his word is not an ethical or moral matter; it has a purely practical basis. An uncertain word destroys and erodes the structure of the personality of the mage. Uncertainty creeps into his soul and compromises his strength. This marks the beginning of the end of the mage.

In the context of what has been said, it is very useful to look at such exercises when any word you say automatically turns into truth. Let it be true, only for one hour, but in an hour, you can do a great deal. Any mage must learn to convince himself, first of all, that everything he says is absolute truth. He is like an actor who is so involved in his role that sometimes he begins to completely identify with his character.

And for those who turn to the mage for help or advice, his word must become law once and for all. The mage should not enter into lengthy discussions with clients, trying to prove something to them, to convince or pander. Doing this only undermines the resolve of the mage himself. Spending your time on empty rhetoric is a terrible thing.

How the mage relates to and communicates to his clients is simple and natural as day replacing night or winter following autumn. First, it can help the mage himself survive. Second, it will help him to improve himself. Third, it is always a reliable defense against attempts to invade his mental state.

RULE NUMBER 4: SECRECY

It is time to talk about the fourth rule; namely, the observance of secrecy. Modern man lives in the age of information and knowledge. Knowledge in our time is the currency over which no inflation has power. New information is found so easily.

What we are talking about here is truly magical, occult knowledge. With knowledge comes power. However, the knowledge that you voluntarily or involuntarily share with someone else is a lost power. For this reason, magic, more than any other human activity, values silence. The necessity for silence and secrecy needs to be considered from several positions.

Let's start with the fact that occult magical practices have a real and quite tangible opponent: the law. Of course in the criminal codes of most developed countries, there are no laws against cursing or binding a person. On the other hand, it's possible that the voodoo doll you made could be accepted into court as evidence of psychological pressure and intimidation, which may entail legal punishment.

In some countries, the conduct of magic in general is prohibited by law. In this case, even a real mage, who has nontraditional knowledge and skills, can be accused of fraud and put behind bars. Unfortunately there are many countries where such activities are generally considered heresy, and in some cases they are punished very cruelly, up to the death penalty.

Anyone, even the most experienced mage, needs to know and remember about such things. After all, a real mage, in the nature of her activity, is a cosmopolitan. She cannot know exactly which country or territory (with the most ridiculous laws) her destiny will lead her to. A real mage does not mourn her place of residence and, of course, never stops her activities, no matter how difficult they are. However, it never hurts to hedge.

Having dealt with the tangible legal side of black magic, let's talk about the intangible, psychological side. Rituals of black magic are best conducted in an atmosphere of semisecrecy. Rather than the object of a spell overtly and consciously knowing magic is being worked on him, it is more effective for the object to wonder about it or be uncertain or learn about it indirectly. How does that look in practice? It's very simple. If a person somehow finds out that a mage is working against him or for him, whether or not he consciously believes in it, on a subconscious level he will be connected to the process. All people are related to each other in some way. For all of us there is such a thing as common sense. Such a person, even if involuntarily, starts to spend his internal energy reserves on attempts to find out what is really going on.

Let the object of influence become aware on some unconscious level, and half the battle is won. The force of the spell will double, and on a purely emotional level, the processes of magical effect will bring you even more pleasure. If you managed to gain the subconscious attention of the object, you can safely proceed to work on him fully, using your own subconscious as the transmitting channel in this case.

A good mage is also a good psychologist, an expert in human souls. She is perfectly aware of what, to whom, when, and in what form to communicate. Her magical work may resemble child's play from the outside, even an innocent prank. After all, adults are the same as children, only wearing a social armor, and they like to be pampered and flattered. It is worth playing along with people to some degree.

If you are not sure of the time and place for a particular rite or ritual, it is better to refuse to hold it or move it to a more convenient time. Even the simplest rite requires maximum concentration of will and effort. You start a mechanism like a blast furnace that you cannot just turn off. And if at that moment an outsider, even the closest person, looks into your room with an innocent question, the consequences may be most unpredictable. You run the risk of angering the dark powers you've awakened, who do not forgive such liberties.

Of course no one is demanding that you close yourself away with one hundred locks, keep outsiders away, or avoid meetings with other people. Reasonable secrecy is, first of all, the ability to balance between mystery and the apparent needs of the moment. Of course this rule does not apply to competing mages.

Also, if you are going to carry out serious rituals to bind a person to yourself, cast a curse, and so on, such plans should be kept in the strictest secrecy from everyone. An exception can only be made for your teacher, if you are a neophyte, and even then not always. Of course you need to be prepared for the fact that your obvious or secret rival, and especially one who is stronger than you, can use special practices to find out about your rites or plans. In some cases he may try to prevent you from doing your work. There's nothing to be done in this case; the strongest will win in such a fight. On the other hand, such magical dueling at a distance is an excellent incentive to achieve new heights in the acquisition of occult knowledge and skills.

It is also necessary to say a few words about the financial side of the issue. You should not take money from a person close to you, even if he is wealthy and can afford it. It will be better if he pays for any materials you need to perform magical activities, such as vodka, bread, or candles.

Cash in its pure form has a very negative effect on the power of magic and contradicts the ancient laws. In any case, such a person will sooner or later pay for everything, but by refusing payment, you will avoid both subjective internal and purely external problems. The halo of mystery also disappears when banal bargaining begins. In the end, a wise mage needs money not to demonstrate her own prestige but so that she won't be distracted by unnecessary trifles, such as worrying whether she has enough money to pay the electric bill, put gas in the car, or buy laundry detergent.

A clear mastering and comprehension of these four basic rules and the ideas of the magical pyramid are necessary for functioning in the world of practical magic, which does not tolerate human weaknesses and unnecessary compromises. To follow these rules is the main task of every neophyte who aspires to become a real mage.

THE LAWS OF MAGIC

Every practitioner understands the laws of magic. I will list a few of them.

- **The law of knowledge.** This is the main law, covering all other principles. Knowledge is power; knowledge gives control and confidence. The more you know about an object, the easier it is to control it.
- **The law of association.** This law's importance is equal to that of the law of knowledge. If different objects have common elements, then they interact through these common elements. Therefore, control over one object gives the practitioner the ability to control the other.
- **The law of similarity.** A precise physical or mental image of an object gives the mage power over the object itself.

- **The law of contact.** Objects that have been in physical contact continue to interact after their separation. Possession of a small particle of another's body, such as nails, hair, or saliva, gives a direct link and access to that person.
- **The law of a name.** The name of an object gives control over it in black magic and sorcery. The name is precise information about a person. In the modern day, the meaning of a name is underestimated, but it is the very essence of a person. A mage who has the name of a victim understands him to his core.
- **The law of the power of words.** There are words that can change internal and external reality. The power of a word is contained in its sound and meaning. Some magical words are ancient names whose meanings are lost.
- **The law of personification.** A mage can personify anything, any phenomenon. The phenomenon acquires a personality as if it were alive. Mages personify winds, clouds, rain, water, the sun and the moon, night and day. They thereby collect, focus, and direct their sorcery.
- **The law of identification.** Through the maximum association of a mage's own elements and the elements of another being, the mage can become that very being. A mage can become so closely identified with another that she possesses that person's knowledge and controls his power.

SPELLS AND WHAT RITUAL WORDS MEAN

Spells are a simplified verbal representation of a desired action. Spells used in magical rituals are associated with the actions performed in the rite. A spell helps to center and aim forces at a given goal. The effectiveness of a spell (as well as of all rituals) depends not only on the forces invoked but also on the personal power of the mage who employs them. In fact, quite often the ritual actions are generally based only on the mage's personal power. The main part of the spell is always concluded with the verbal formula "So be it!" In the old days "So shall it be!" and "It shall!" were more common. And before that, many used "Alatyr!"

At times, mages would end the spell with the word *amen*. Followers of the so-called blasphemous path of black magic end their spells with the word *nema*—amen spelled or said backward. They say the word in imitation of church prayers that end with amen. By doing so, they express their contempt for God. For them, the word *nema* means both "I despise you, God" and "So be it!"

THE ALATYR-STONE

An Alatyr-stone is a sacred stone for pagan Slavs. It is mentioned in many legends, myths, folktales, and fairy tales and used in spells. An Alatyr-stone can be considered a cult stone or a cult object. The word *altar* comes directly from Alatyr.

Alatyr, the father of all stones, is both small and powerful, cold and combustible. He is often endowed with healing powers. The stone contains great wisdom and all knowledge and has a creative, demiurgic, and life-giving power. There is a mighty power both in the stone itself and under it: healing rivers flow from beneath the stone.

There are still disputes about how this object originated and where it is located. Judging by various legends, the Alatyr-stone appeared at the very beginning of time and was honored by the gods themselves. According to one version, the stone fell from the sky. In another version, Svarog brought it to the land from the bottom of the sea. It may be located in the middle of the sea, in the center of the world, or the center of the universe. According to other sources, the stone is located at the entrance to the underworld or afterworld, on the riverbank. According to a third version, the stone is located on a sacred mountain. The eastern and southern Slavs believed that the Alatyr-stone lies in Iria (the

Slavic paradise) under Pradub (the Tree of Life) and was created by Rod (the Source, Creator God) from an egg.

Rod actually represents the monotheistic religion of the ancient Slavs. Although there are many Slavic gods, Rod is portrayed as a kind of god that you may encounter in monotheistic religion today. Rod also fits into the scheme of Nietzsche's God, who had existed to create the world and form the principles of the universe. When he had finished his goal, he could disappear or die. Rod becomes a principle and ceases to appear as God, ceases to meddle in the lives of mortals and gods directly, but he is always present, and the principles that he represents affect everyone. He is in everything; in fact, he is the basis of everything. Everything visible and invisible depicts Rod.

Rod created the stone Alatyr, which poured the milk of life, and from that milk Mother Earth and the milky ocean were created. Alatyr remained on the milky ocean bottom, and from the sea foam the duck Sveta was created, who gave the birth to many other gods. Perun, the god of thunder and lightning, rested on the Alatyr-stone every winter.

Another account says that Alatyr is the altar stone of the god Baal. Baal, also known as Bel or Baloo, is an ancient god of the Semitic peoples of the Mediterranean coast. He was distinguished by his power and cruelty. Some historians believe he was the first formal global patron god. Baal's sphere of influence was extremely broad in the cultures where he held the dominant position. He was a god of thunder, similar to the ancient Greek Zeus or Roman Jupiter. He patronized the sunshine, and in the heyday of the Phoenician culture, he protected seafarers and traders. In a religious sense, this Phoenician and Chaldean god came before all else.

Later the Romans and Greeks made additional connections, the most important of which was identifying Baal with Kronos, or Saturn, the Titan that Zeus and other Greek gods fought. In this myth is played out the large-scale confrontation of these two cultures,

Semitic and Greco-Roman. Subsequently, when the foundations of Judaism began to be laid, the cult of Baal was persecuted by the first Jewish prophets. The most famous such event is the biblical prophet Elijah killing all the priests of Baal. He is best known for eradicating paganism and his ascension to heaven while alive. Baal was demonized in connection with this large-scale struggle. Later Baal became Beelzebub, from the Greek word *beelzeboub,* derived from the Hebrew *ba'al-z'bub,* meaning "lord of the flies," or the devil. (*Baal* means "lord," and *z'bhubh,* "fly.")

The Russians and Slavs began to call Baal Veles,* who is, as noted earlier, the Slavic god of earth, waters, forests, and the underworld. The names of Veles include Vaal-Gad, Vaal Pehar or Fehar, Vaal-Zamen, Vaal Zephon, and finally Vaal Zeewood (Baal-Fly), a name given to the god Vaal-Zamen. The Slavic name Beloe or Bela, which means "white," is similar to Baal. Friedrich Karl Vollmer says that the Babylonians called the sun by this name.

SORCERY BOOKS OR BOOKS OF SHADOWS

Mages have always kept sorcery notebooks or so-called books of shadows for personal use. Each mage creates a scripture or receives it from his teacher. Such books can also be used to create sorcery communities. Recipients of a sorcery book, over time and as they gain experience and develop their own practices, supplement the books with new methods. Only effective and proven techniques are recorded in the book, with one major rite per page. Mages often have auxiliary books that contain necessary but less-important knowledge useful in the practice of sorcery.

Ideally such a book is made by hand by sewing together sheets

---

*Veles has a number of words connected to it, including *vel* (drive), *val* (shaft), *vol* (ox), *bel* (white), *bal* (ball), and *bol* (bole).

impregnated with powerful herbs into a leather cover. The closure must be a clasp, a buckle, or ties. Many mages prefer to add droplets of their own blood and ground herbs to the ink with which they write. This is how mages created books in ancient times. Modern-day mages usually omit these conventions and instead order the production of books from the masters of such crafts.

Mages protect their books with various spells so that an outsider experiences discomfort or even perishes if he picks up such a book (he cannot open it or read it without the permission of the owner). Mages often attach "watchmen" demons or dead souls to a book to protect it. There can be kind of an initiation ritual performed at a place of power to keep this book protected. *No one* will be able to read it. They often place protective signs or the seals of their demon patrons on the cover of the book.

PRACTICES OF MAGES

Mages are powerful and not talkative. They behave with dignity in any situation. There is a folk belief that the souls of dead mages who are not laid to rest will become magpies (ravens). As birds, they help living mages find the most suitable places for sorcery in forests and cemeteries.

Mages do not go to church, but they do sometimes visit them for blasphemous church sorcery. Mages usually try to leave such places quickly, as churches often cause them to become ill. In the old days, mages invariably demonstrated their dislike of people on major Orthodox holidays, such as Christmas, the Baptism, Easter, and so on. At a time when everyone was at a church service, mages would lock themselves in their huts in protest. They would loudly read their sorcery literature, or have fun, drink, swear, and play balalaikas (Russian traditional musical instrument). They behaved immorally to prove their devotion to the Unclean Forces. As noted previously, natural mages can receive information directly from the Unclean Forces. Satan himself does not teach, according to common belief. Demons who serve mages provide them with information through visions (clairvoyance), knowledge (clairgnosis), and hearing (clairaudience).

Black magic is a difficult and dangerous craft, and not everyone is able to learn it. Those who attempt it without a gift or knowledge may simply perish. It is believed that if a mage goes a month without casting a curse or spell on anyone, he will become ill. The evil spirits will punish him for his inactivity. The mage may even lose his life. Many times a witch will send demons to weave ropes of sand to keep them busy and keep them away for a while.

THE BEST TIME FOR SORCERY

Dark magic is best performed from sunset to dawn of the next day. The optimal and most favorable time is between midnight and 3 a.m. (known as the witching hour). The waning moon as it sets is also a most effective time for conducting rituals of a dark nature, such as curses, and is the best time to lift spells cast by other mages. Perform purification and weight loss rituals under the waning moon. Positive rituals (for love, beauty, wealth, protection, etc.) are best conducted under the waxing moon. Of course if there is urgent need, the lunar cycle can be disregarded, but the ritual will be significantly weakened.

If a rite is aimed at forgetting the past, you should perform it at sunrise (for example, purification). Perform a rite after sunset if your goal is to influence the future. It a good idea for novices to also take into account the male days (Monday, Tuesday, Thursday) and female days (Wednesday, Saturday, Friday), especially for healing and cleansing rituals. (In the Russian language the days fall into these gender divisions; Sunday is considered neuter gender.)

To be most effective, mages select the day and hour of the rite according to the well-known table of planetary days and hours.

THE POWER OF CROSSROADS

Crossroads, such as intersections and forks, symbolize the difficulty of choice. The crossroads is the place where you ask: Which road should I take? Crossroads also symbolize uncertainty and loss of hope and longing for a lost shepherd, leader, or guide. In many cultures, a crossroads is a meeting place with transcendental forces (gods, spirits, the dead). The symbolism of the crossroads is like that of a door, marking the transition from the old to the new, from the earthly to the otherworldly.

Crossroads figure prominently in many cultures and traditions. Among African tribes, crossroads are often the place of ritual ceremonies. In Hinduism, the crossroads acted as a refuge for demons. The Romans prayed to household gods at crossroads. In ancient Rome, apart from the *lares,* patrons of domestic life, there were road gods, which were called *Lares compitales.* They guarded the wanderer from evil forces, and offerings to these road gods were made at crossroads as well.

For the ancient Greeks, crossroads bring a meeting with destiny. Statues of Hermes-Psychopomp, a spirit guide, stood at the crossroads. The god Hermes had many characteristics and represented many things. Hermes was the Olympic god of farmers and farms, travelers and hospitality, roads and trade, theft and love, prophecies and diplomacy, astronomy and astrology. He was also a god of science and wisdom, of art, of speech, of hope. And, most importantly, "God of writing." He was the keeper of the crossroads and the entrances of houses. He protected the trade, the travelers, and the athletes. He had another talent though.

He was Jupiter's personal messenger, as well as the guide of the dead who led the souls down into the underworld. This last task required the fleet-footed Hermes to be able to cross the worlds with ease, which probably explains why he is also the god of crossing the border. His job was also to lead the souls of the dead to the entrance of Hades, where they waited for Harrodas to take them. Hermes was the only Olympian god able to visit Heaven, Earth, *and* Hades, which he enjoyed bragging about to the other gods.

According to a Greek myth, the young Hercules sat at a crossroads, reflecting on his fate. It was then that the goddesses Arete (virtue) and Hedone (pleasure) appeared before him. The first offered the future hero a life full of difficulties and patience, which led to immortality; the second offered a path to joy and luxury. Hercules chose the first. In the famous Greek myth of Oedipus, it was at the crossroads that he met his father, whom he had never seen before and did not recognize, and killed him as the result of a quarrel.

The ancient Greeks believed that the three-headed goddess Hecate, who is associated with the realm of the dead and is the patroness of mages, ghosts, and witchcraft, appeared on clear nights in places where three roads converge. She is accompanied by spirits and howling phantom dogs. The Greeks left food at the crossroads for her. They turned to Hecate for help if someone was insane, because it was believed that the spirits of the dead sent this disease to mortals.

Ancient crossroads were considered a symbol of the triple epiphany, combining three principles: active (good), neutral (productive or useful), and passive (harmful). For example, Hecate shows the threefold aspect of a deity, embodying maiden, mother, and crone, and birth, fecundity, and death, as well as earth, sea, and sky. The crossroads is the symbol of choice in general and, in particular, the choice between life and death, as well as the sign of the transition from one space to another. As such, the crossroads is endowed with an ambivalent meaning. On the one hand, this place was sacred. In Christianity, a crossroads, likened to a cross in its form, became the place of veneration of Christ. In the Middle Ages, crucifixes were placed at the crossroads of main roads to protect them from the presence of evil spirits. Christians erected crosses, chapels, and Madonna and other statues at crossroads.

On the other hand, the crossroads was considered to be the focus of harmful, impure forces. At the crossroads, witchcraft rituals were performed. In Europe, crossroads were seen as meeting places for mages and evil spirits. In Slavic mythology, the crossroads was considered a home for devils. Magical rituals often sought protection from the devil and demons at crossroads. In addition, the crossroads suggests the need to be particularly sensitive and cautious, because robbers often arrange ambushes at crossroads.

In Europe, there was a belief that you are likely to meet all kinds of playful creatures at the crossroads, including mages, who like to knock people off the right path. According to popular beliefs, ghosts also love crossroads. In German folklore there is a story about a crossroad in the town of Schleswig that a ghost rider frequents. The neck of the rider's horse stretches across the road and does not allow travelers to pass.

A legend popular in Pomerania, on the border of Poland and Germany, says that a traveler once stopped at night on a crossroads and saw a dark figure in front of him wearing long clothes and wooden shoes. To the traveler's full amazement, the mysterious figure followed him home and settled in his house. Eventually this man gathered his courage and spoke to the ghost. He asked the poor fellow to go with him to the cemetery so that he could say a few prayers and help the ghost find eternal peace.

The spirits of the deceased appear near crossroads on the eve of All Saints' Day (October 31), which was first a pagan and then a Christian holiday. On this day the barrier dividing the two worlds is believed to be the thinnest. Residents of Wales believe that a large number of spirits go to the crossroads on this night. In Europe, there are beliefs that on the eve of All Saints' Day the deceased form processions heading toward the homes of their living relatives, and a person who stands at a crossroads and puts his chin on a forked stick can see these processions.

In other cases, special spells make it possible to summon the spirits of the deceased to the crossroads. According to one ancient Danish rite, the person who needed to summon a spirit should go out at midnight on the eve of All Saints' Day to the crossroads and stand inside a square formed by wagons. At the mention of his name, the ghost would appear and answer three questions.

Another belief was that some rituals performed at a crossroads on certain days (in particular on the eve of All Saints' Day) allow you to find out in advance who will die in the near future. For example, Welshmen believed that if a person went to the crossroads and listened to "the wind blowing over the feet of the dead" (the east wind), he would be able to hear sighs in those houses where people would die in the coming year. The Highlanders of Scotland had a similar belief: if you sat on a three-legged chair at a crossroads, at midnight you would hear the names of those who were doomed to die in the near future. In German folklore, the same type of ritual was performed at the crossroads between eleven o'clock and midnight on Christmas Eve or on the eve of All Saints' Day.

Traveling through crossroads had special significance in funeral rites. According to one ancient Welsh custom, the deceased were laid on the ground at every crossroads and prayers were read over them on the way from the house to the cemetery. Perhaps this was done to protect the deceased from evil spirits who chose such places for their visits and also, perhaps, to prevent the ghost of the deceased from returning to the house and interfering with the living. In Hesse, a central state in Germany, it was believed that the specter of the deceased would not return to the house if the dishes that belonged to him were broken at the crossroads. In Finland, participants of the funeral processions took the land from each crossroads they passed by and then scattered the land across the fields, thus protecting themselves from witchcraft (and ensuring a good harvest).

For many peoples, suicides were buried at intersections of roads. However, there are no intelligible explanations about this practice. Suicides were not allowed to be buried in Christian cemeteries. Perhaps this tradition is related to the fact that the cross formed by crossroads is associated with the consecrated ground of Christian cemeteries (where, as is known, no suicides were buried), or perhaps the reason for this is the desire to use the supernatural properties of intersections to prevent suicides from returning to life.

In many cultures, people believe that crossroads provide protection from ghosts. For example, one fairly common German superstition is that spirits cannot cross crossroads; thus, a person chased by a ghost or demonic being could shake his pursuer at a crossroads. As soon as the pursued person reached the crossroads, the spirit disappeared, issuing a completely inhuman scream. Similarly, the Irish believed that at the crossroads, fairy magic did not work and that mortals abducted by fairies could regain their freedom in such places.

Ancient Germans brought captured robbers to crossroads as a sacrifice to their gods, turning these places into a kind of scaffold. In medieval Germany, trials often took place at crossroads. According to later German law, it was legal to exact punishments at crossroads. In the Middle Ages, they traditionally buried executed criminals and those accused of witchcraft or suspected of vampirism at crossroads. The last, as a rule, were pierced through the chest with an aspen stake.

As mentioned earlier, crossroads are among the places on Earth's surface favored by demons, where they perform their works. Mages go to crossroads to make offerings to demons and ask for their help in performing spells. The standard crossroads is the intersection of two roads, suitable for almost any ritual. Crossroads where three roads cross at one

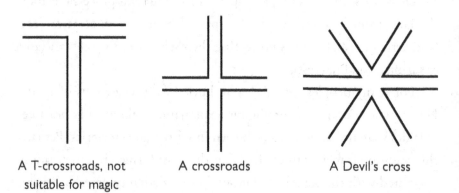

A T-crossroads, not suitable for magic

A crossroads

A Devil's cross

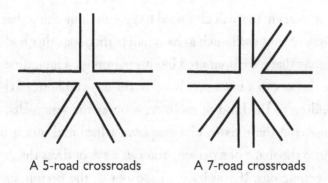

A 5-road crossroads   A 7-road crossroads

point and go in different directions at about the same angle are very good for witchcraft. (T-junctions are not suitable for witchcraft. You can ignore them; they are, in fact, not even crossroads.) Mages seek the crossroads of three roads for certain works (that is, an intersection that diverges on six sides). Such crossroads are called the Devil's Cross in the tradition of black magic and can be used to sell souls and to evoke demons and send them after people. Sometimes mages use more complex crossroads. There are five- and seven-road crossroads that are very strong, but they are not easy to find.

DOLLS FOR MAGICAL WORK

A doll is a tool of the mage. It is a means of influencing the victim of witchcraft from a distance. The doll is also called a puppet of the enemy. It is filled with rage and made to match the victim. Dolls are widely used in magic to exert influence over people. With the help of the doll you can not only curse and cast black magic but also heal, cast protective spells at a distance, and control a person in every possible way.

The doll is often made from wax, but you can make it from many other materials, such as clay, dough, and dry grass, or it can be sewn from the clothes of the intended victim. To make a wax doll, you need pure wax, such as beeswax or a plant wax (palm, bayberry, or soybean), not paraffin or stearin. You will also need to procure something that belongs to the target of your spell, such as hair, nail parings, or other bodily material or objects that have been used by this person for a long time.

Place the wax in a hot water bath on the day and hour of the planet corresponding to the kind of spell. As soon as the wax melts, add the organic material (hair, nails, blood, sperm, saliva) and mix it in. Form the wax into the shape of a person. You can wrap or dress the doll in the personal belongings. If you have a headshot of the person, affix it on the doll's face, which will make the doll resemble the person even more. After you have finished making the doll, say: "I bring you to life and dub you [name of person]."

Now you can safely carry out almost any ritual you know on the figure, knowing that the real person will experience whatever happens to it.

OFFERINGS

In magic, the term *offering* refers to a whole class of rituals, most of which are aimed at getting rid of something negative, such as an offering against death, an offering against a serious illness, or an offering against imprisonment. The main purpose and meaning of these rituals are to make an offering on behalf of a person to solve his problems. Masters only make an offering to Death, for example, when a client is dying, and traditional medical treatment may not help him in time. The master makes the offering to buy the client additional time until he can get back on his feet or at least be stabilized. A *tribute* is a kind of payment to certain forces to ask for help when executing a task. A tribute is a gratitude to mitigate or neutralize the side effect of the ritual, which is usually called the *magical recoil*.

Another nuance about offerings—no matter what we bring to the gods, it is important *how* we bring it. If a certain god or spirit loves a certain set of objects, and in the absence of this we brought a piece of bread or something else, but from the heart, the gods will accept this offering. Because it is not the subject of the offering itself that is important but rather the feeling of gratitude, love of the gods, that is important. This is the energy from which they feed. Another way to do it is to place an ad in the newspaper thanking a specific god, spirit, or demon, so that his name and glory will grow.

If you don't make an offering, your spell or ritual is likely to be ineffective. For example, say that you want to bewitch a loved one: you go to a cemetery, perform the ritual and appeal to the necessary forces for aid, and leave—and then wonder why the opposite of what you wanted happened or nothing happened at all. Nothing happened because you came to the home of the spirits (the cemetery) and used their power but gave nothing in return. You have to pay for what you get, anywhere and everywhere; nothing is free. (For more on cemetery offerings, see "Greeting and Offering Gifts to the Dead" in chapter 6.)

Forces (the cluster of cemetery energy), unlike spirits, are not personified. Offerings are rarely given in material goods. As a rule, the forces take part of your energy in return for their help. Therefore, so that a mage can work effectively with the forces and at the same time not taint his health, he must have sufficient power and energy and be able to quickly replenish himself.

SACRIFICES

In Russian black magic, mages traditionally sacrifice roosters to the Unclean Forces (for important rituals). Evil spirits become active late in the evening, when darkness falls with the last cry of the rooster. They hide in the morning with the rooster's first cry. A rooster will never sleep through dawn and will never miss dusk.

The Unclean Forces cannot touch and cope with an adult rooster, because it has an angelic rank given by God himself. The comb on its head is no less than an angelic crown. The Unclean Forces hate and fear roosters so intensely that rooster blood is their favorite treat. Both roosters and hens are used for sacrifices as hens give life to roosters. The Unclean Forces also like sacrifices in the form of white doves as they personify the Holy Spirit. They are used mainly for witchcraft initiations at the moment of the renunciation of God, as well as the blood of white lambs (representative of the Lamb of God or Jesus Christ), which is used mainly for ceremonies of rejuvenation.

Traditionally it is forbidden to use dogs, cats, rams, goats, kids, crows, ravens, magpies, toads, frogs, and snakes. These animals and other birds and amphibians are sacred. Snakes, toads, and frogs are only occasionally used as offerings in some witchcraft. As a rule, in the sacrificial work carried out in places of power, the animals are slaughtered with a bewitched knife and their blood is spilled onto the ground.

The Bewitched Knife

A necessary item of a mage is a bewitched knife or ritual knife. These knives are necessary for sorcerers and witches to make bloody sacrifices as well as perform other work.

The ritual knife is kept separately, is not given to anyone, and is not shown to anyone. Sorcerers and witches buy their ritual knives from the best craftsmen of blacksmithing, preferring the best grades of steel. They do not negotiate on price. The handles and the sheathes of knives are made by masters of joinery from the best varieties of black wood or oak or walnut, which are further darkened by black staining. The sheath is made of dark, durable leather stitched with rough black natural threads. The handle of the witch's knife is arranged in such a way that the witch's hand does not come in contact with any of the metal of the knife as she wields it for her work. The blade's handle should be provided with a small crossbar to prevent the brush from slipping off the handle when using the knife in a stabbing motion.

Sorcerers and witches engaged in witchcraft as a profession sometimes have several additional knives for various practical purposes. For example: sacrificial knifes for Gods or entities, sacrificial knives for clients to gods or entities, knives for personal magical use, and so on. Sometimes witches used disposable knives for practical purposes. A master who practices old-world witchcraft knows how many knives he or she needs and the purpose of each. Such knives are charged separately in a special way by the Unclean Force.

Depending on the ritual, the body of the sacrificial animal is either left near where the ritual took place or buried there. The sacrifice may also be thrown or fed to the object of influence. In some cases, the remains may be used for food. In rare cases (for example, offerings against death), the sacrifice is buried alive in the ground. In other cases, the sacrificial animal is left alive in the place of power. Three days are required before sacrificing an animal (the animal is not caged or leashed and is generously fed and cared for), and before the work is done, the victim is bathed in fresh water (paws, beak, hooves, and snouts are washed). The animal should not be tied up when it is given in sacrifice but only firmly held. If the sacrifice manages to break free, then it means that the Unclean Forces do not accept the sacrifice.

There are some rules for sacrificial work: a mage is not allowed to leave his blood, hair, or saliva on the sacrifice or at the place of the ritual.

HOW TO SUMMON DEMONS AND WHY

Demons fulfill certain roles. A mage who hopes to get a demon's aid must take special action. If your goal is to make a demon appear, the process is a simple one. You have to make a sacrifice at the crossroads. You must leave or bury a black chicken and read the appropriate spell. But, if the goal is for him to obey, very complex rituals are needed.

Calling a demon must be in compliance with the laws of the infernal world. The ritual must be conducted in the correct sequence. Demon summoning rituals are complex. Each demon has its own seal, signs, and true name. The seal not only carries information about the demon but also reflects the essence of the demonologist. Seals are individual and very diverse. They are used by demons of all levels. When you summon a lesser demon, you will use simple and closed seals. Professional mages use combined seals when making contact with the otherworld.

However, it would be a mistake to think that knowledge of the ritual and the magical formula is sufficient to summon and control a demon. A true demonologist knows that the formula varies depending on the day of the week, the time of day, the location of the summons, and the people present. The slightest mistake can and most likely will be fatal. To form a contract with a fallen angel, you need to know as many of his secret names as possible, as well as his purpose, title, and favorite worlds. Each demon has a particular area of expertise for which he is equipped to help.

To perform the ritual, you need a black rooster, standing water, incense, and mirrors. A pentagram is a typical attribute of the ritual; it gives time for negotiations. Some authors argue that this is also the simplest and most effective way to get a demon to keep his word. You can do everything correctly, but only the demon can decide how to appear before you or whether to appear at all. Do not bow down before him and do not imagine yourself above him. Demons are wayward and require special respect but not slavish obedience.

Mistakes can occur during rituals that lead to the death of amateurs. The most innocuous thing that can happen to you is a loss of consciousness or a heart attack. Therefore, my strong advice to you is not to meddle in this kind of magic. Summoning a demon is detrimental to the soul. You must be aware of this and not expect a different outcome. Contact a black mage for help.

6

PRINCIPLES OF
CEMETERY MAGIC

Cemeteries are the strongest places of power and can be used for both good and evil. Black magic practitioners spend an enormous amount of time working in them. Even ordinary people can feel the power of a cemetery. No other place causes people's moods to change so suddenly. Most people are afraid of cemeteries and are eager to leave. Some inexplicable fear haunts anyone who goes into a cemetery in the evening.

The soul leaves the body at the time of death but remains attached to the place where the body is buried. That is why cemeteries are believed to be inhabited by many spirits. Those spirits, if properly invoked, are able to fulfill any request or desire.

A cemetery is like a city of the dead, similar in size and population to a small town. It has both large and small portals or gates: the central entrance and additional entranceways. It is enclosed by a wall or fence that separates the world of the living from the world of the dead. In the churchyard itself are crossroads, both marked and unmarked graves, chapels, and other altars.

In recent times, there has been a change in the way cemeteries are perceived, both by ordinary people and by mages. They began to be perceived as a kind of portal to the afterlife, to a hell inhabited by all kinds of demons. When a mage works in a cemetery he plunges into dark waters, into another reality, the underworld, and completely changes his consciousness.

In fact, cemeteries themselves do not carry heavy energy. In the end, the whole of our planet is a great, big cemetery, where all the people and other life-forms who have lived and died now rest. But many, perhaps most, people no longer believe that death is a transition to another stage, a new level: according to them, death is the absolute end of existence. For this reason, almost every visitor to the cemetery goes there with heavy thoughts and leaves his negative energy behind.

Cemeteries are full of extraordinary power and energy that can be used to achieve sorcery, but to use this power and achieve your goals, you must know the principles of sorcery. You must observe the rules of work in cemeteries that come from the same principles. Mages going to work in the cemetery observe certain rules even on the way to the cemetery. Once they enter its territory they perform certain actions, say certain words, and make offerings. They also give certain greetings with explanations and offerings for the mistress of the cemeteries. These actions are also carried out on cemetery land. Over time, with experience, mages lose their fear of the cemetery and graves.

You must be very respectful of the cemetery and everything related to it. Not all graves are suitable for sorcery work. Only the active ones are ready for use (see page 87).

A mage, when he comes to the cemetery, usually seeks a grave of the same name given to him by someone asking for help or someone who wishes another ill. He establishes contact with the soul of the deceased. The heavy, depressive energy of the churchyard is used to achieve the goal. What he seeks to do, whether it is a love spell or a curse, is not so important. A cemetery can even work to reduce someone's negative energy, as like attracts like. Some of the people buried in a cemetery are the forgotten or unmourned dead because they were laid to rest without funeral rites. These people can be anonymous corpses or mages buried as anyone else would be.

A variety of offerings are made at the cemetery, as they are in other places of power, such as coins, tobacco, liquor, and blood sacrifices. Contrary to popular belief, mages do not use food as an offering to the dead. The dead aren't hungry. They do not make offerings of blood and meat because it's just ridiculous! The forces are not dogs or wolves. The energy of the blood comes out when the offering is sacrificed. After this brief moment, the blood is just liquid and the meat is just meat.

Mages work not only at graves in the cemetery but also at the cemetery crossroads, where they address the bloodthirsty demons. They placate them with various gifts. Like any other evil spirits, they respond best to blood sacrifices. Less often, mages conduct sorcery at cemetery fences and under cemetery trees. After mages finish their work in cemeteries, they leave and say certain sentences as they cross its boundaries. They also follow certain rules to the very threshold of their home, and upon returning they perform certain procedures for self-cleansing.

To begin working in a cemetery, you need to understand and know some features of the work. You need to know how to properly bring offerings and sacrifices to the cemetery. You need to know that demons live at the cemetery crossroads. As you leave, you need to leave a second offering. You also need to know to make offerings both at the grave and to the mistress of the cemeteries.

CHOOSING A GRAVE

In the tradition of black magic, not all graves are suitable for sorcery. Only the graves of those dead whose souls who await the Last Judgment and have not yet been swallowed up by either the Unclean Forces or God are suitable. While they await their fate, these souls are tied to the burial place of their bodies and periodically return to their gravesites at night.

An experienced mage will be able to select the necessary grave for work relying on his vision (clairvoyance, clairgnosis, and clairaudience). Novices usually choose active graves according to the following principles, but experienced mages also often use the following signs. An active grave attracts animals. If crows, ravens, magpies, or other birds are watching a grave or circling over it, this is a clear sign of activity. Cats, dogs, and other animals also like to wander near active graves. One of the best signs of a grave's activeness is seeing a cat on it. Sometimes there are dead trees on or next to an active grave. Often trees near or on a grave grow in curves and ugly shapes. If you feel an oppressive atmosphere or discomfort as you walk through the cemetery, this is also a sign of activity. In the summer, the graves will be covered in withered, yellow grass. Any vegetation that grows on them will do so with reluctance. In winter, the snow on an active grave will look crushed and gray. If there are feathers or cat, dog, or bird tracks, the grave is suitable for work. Watch for the movement of trees. The swaying of treetops and branches can indicate an active grave. On active graves, gravestones, even very large and new ones, have many cracks and natural wear. The images on such graves fade faster, lose brightness, and disappear (if there is an image). Crosses on active graves rot quickly and very often break. They may even fall to the ground. Harmful weeds usually grow on active graves.

The burial places of suicides, murderers, murder victims, and apostates (including defrocked priests) are admirably suited for sorcery. In the old days, suicides, murderers, and deceased mages were often not buried in common cemeteries. The custom was to bury them behind the cemetery fence or at the site of their death and to not remember or grieve for them. The graves of stillborn infants and unbaptized infants are also admirably suited for certain rituals, as are those of young people and children. Family graves are often good for sowing disagreement and madness in a home. In small village cemeteries, the seventh, ninth, and thirteenth unnamed graves in the far left corner of the cemetery are often very good for sorcery work. They can be used to cast severe, fatal curses.

In most cases, unmarked graves are used for serious curses

(including death curses), and sometimes, for the destructive aspect of love magic (including breakup spells). Very often these spirits show aggression, and working with them is difficult and energy intensive, especially for beginners. It is also worth noting that when it comes to an unmarked grave, you should use an old, poorly kept grave with a lopsided tombstone with no name, not a recently buried person. Working with the graves of suicides requires even greater caution. The work is complex and should be left to masters. As a rule, suicides are offered blood sacrifices.

At children's graves, especially those of infants, you should only conduct rituals that specifically call for their use. If the rite does not indicate a child's grave but simply mentions the use of a particular name, it should be carried out at the grave of an adult of the same name. Usually child and infant graves are used for severe curses of sickness, death, insanity, and addiction.

Perhaps the most dangerous and complex grave is that of a mage. Only a very experienced and strong master can work with such a grave. The practitioner must first have experience holding various special rituals before attempting to work with a mage's grave (see "A Contract with a Mage" in chapter 7). An unskillful approach to such a grave can lead to hefty consequences, such as a premature death for the practitioner or his or her family.

When choosing a grave for a ritual, you must learn to sense whether the deceased wants to help. Keep in mind that there are graves protected against sorcery (see "To Seal a Grave against a Mage" in chapter 7). Those who rest there will not help. Ask or sense their feelings like this: Stand at the head of the grave facing the tombstone. Close your eyes, stretch your palms forward, and ask in a whisper if the deceased would be willing to help you. If you feel warm and calm, then the deceased agrees. If you feel cold, anxious, or fearful, then the deceased does not agree. You must look for another grave for the ritual.

GREETING AND OFFERING GIFTS TO THE DEAD

The general rule when starting work with a grave, whether unnamed or not, is that you must greet and ask the permission of the deceased. As you enter a cemetery, you must raise your voice in greeting to the inhabitants of the kingdom of the dead. Bring several pennies and pour vodka on the ground in front of you three times.

When you perform a ritual on a grave, always bring the deceased an offering or gift. There are many types of offerings that you can make at graves, depending on the deceased in question. If a specific offering is not stipulated in a ritual, alcohol (usually vodka or rum, sometimes sweet wine or red wine, depending on the work the mage is doing) and sweets (sugar, honey, cookies, candies) can serve as universal offerings. The dead accept sweets willingly. Other offerings include coins (silver colored and pennies), tobacco (cigarettes, pipe, cigars), bread, and gold and other jewelry. For blood sacrifices, a black hen or rooster is preferable; less often white pigeons or doves and lambs are used. (For more on sacrifices, see "Sacrifices" in chapter 5.)

When you perform a ritual at the crossroads, you must also always leave an offering in the form of coins, vodka, lit cigars, and the same types of food as enumerated above. Offerings are also left at a cemetery crossroads immediately after performing a ceremony at a grave.

For those who died as adults, you can bring tobacco, vodka, or rum (the most important thing is the quality of alcohol and strength; do not bring weak liquor). For a child's grave, you must offer different things: jam, sweets, or toys. Children who leave their bodies early did not have a good time during life. You must show respect to all spirits, even to those who are small. A child's spirit lives in a cemetery for centuries and sees a great deal.

Do not take anything from the cemetery, and do not perform other works from the grave without an offering. Otherwise the dead will become angry and draw you to where they are. Do not tempt fate.

HOW TO RECITE SPELLS

You should memorize the spell by heart. In extreme cases, you can rewrite the spell by hand and read it off a sheet of paper. You must pronounce the text without hesitation, pauses, or distortion. Unless otherwise instructed, read all spells while facing west. You need to know how many times to read the spell. If you're not certain, read it an odd number of times: once, three times, seven times, or nine times (trust your senses in that case). Keep track of the number of repetitions in your mind. Don't use your fingers to count them off! If the number of repetitions is large, you can keep track with matches and move them after each iteration. When mages perform any magical actions, including reciting spells, they often have a feeling that someone is watching them, but they must not turn around no matter what. They will not see anyone, and their actions will be less effective.

MATERIALS FOR RITUALS

You must always buy new materials for the ritual. Aside from magical instruments (such as a ritual knife), the material that you use for a ritual should not have a personal relationship with you and should not contain your energy. For example, you should not make dolls from your own clothing.

Use only candles made from beeswax or plants, the kind that are suitable for church, although church candles are not used in all rituals. Church candles need to be turned upside down for certain spells and rituals. You cannot blow out any candles! You must extinguish them with your fingers, or with a device meant for that purpose.

If a photograph is needed in the ritual, there should not be any other person in the photograph besides the one on which the work is done. It is strictly forbidden to use a photo with several people. The person should not have his or her arms crossed or be wearing sunglasses.

Certain objects are very powerful. You can work many marvelous deeds with the noose of a man who hanged himself. It has enough power for three spells and curses a day, including for wealth and career success. Wastewater from bathing the deceased can be used in powerful rituals, both for ferocious curses and strong purifications. It can cure terrible disease.

If you take water from a cemetery puddle (so-called dead water), you must give the mistress of the cemeteries an offering. You must do the same if you take flowers from a grave (which can be used in curses). If you take a bone from the ground, you may keep it, but do not take any fabric. Leave a penny on the same spot.

DAYS OF REVERENCE AT THE CEMETERY

Regardless of your goal when performing magic, if you perform rituals in a cemetery, you must make an offering at the cemetery on certain days so as to ensure that the ritual will take effect on time and with maximum force. Days of reverence to the masters of the churchyard fall on January 7, February 19, April 8, May 24, June 3, July 1, September 21, October 28, and November 26. (For optimal times to perform sorcery, see "The Best Time for Sorcery" in chapter 5.)

In the modern day, you need to go to the cemetery and leave an offering. You must ask for patronage, protection, and help from the mistress of the cemeteries. It is better to leave offerings at the crossroads or at big, old cemetery trees. At the entrance to the cemetery, you must immediately appeal to the mistress of the cemeteries. Ask for her suggestion as to who will help you in your practice or ritual. Then try to sense what she tells you or look for her signs.

In addition to the mistress of the cemeteries, a mage will encounter many other forces. Offerings to the mistress include wine, chocolate, cookies, flowers, candies, a candle, honey, jewelry, and scarves. If you stick to these days and give all that is listed, the mistress of the cemeteries will favor you and protect you against your enemies for the rest of your life.

If you do not cry or scream when you work with the dead, they will do everything you ask them to. If you do cry or scream, they will punish you. Do your work and remain quiet. Do not be afraid of the dead. They live their own life after the grave, and if your sorcery is successful, none of them will touch you or cling to you. Do not tremble in the cemetery; do not show fear. Fear is weakness. Be confident in yourself and your power!

7

CEMETERY SPELLS

LOVE MAGIC IN THE CEMETERY

Love spells are rituals aimed at evoking a feeling of love. First of all, the spell is a rite that acts on a person on a subconscious level. As a result, he has a desire to be near the person who performs the rite or the one who orders it to take place. With the help of love spells, you can reunite with a loved one or find a loved one for the first time, develop love and passion, improve relations between lovers, create a family, create a good climate in a family, and remove negative influences aimed at loneliness. There are a huge number of love spells that can be used to bewitch a loved one. There are all kinds of spells and charms, love drinks and potions, and ties and bindings to awaken sexual desires. The strongest group of spells includes the black spell, the cemetery spell, and the blood spell.

There are several ways to cast a spell, such as the following:

1. Through food and drinks (magical and organic)
2. Through personal belongings (magical)
3. Through plants, such as herbs and flowers, and trees (magical)
4. Through minerals (magical)
5. With the help of natural phenomena; spells on snow, rain, rainbows, thunder, lightning, and at dawn and dusk (magical)

6. Through the powers of the moon and the sun (magical)
7. Through a prayerful appeal to the egregor of your religion or tradition (magical)

Remember, a love spell must be cast only when you are absolutely sure that you desire the person you want to bewitch. If you cast the spell out of curiosity or to cause someone pain, it will not work at full strength. Perfection of the human spirit is possible thanks only to the harmonization of opposing principles in human nature and the universe as a whole.

✿ SEWING IN THE CEMETERY

What you need: a thread spool; needle and thread; an offering of cookies, honey, and pennies; a piece of clothing from your beloved; buttons; seven branches of wormwood; a bottle of wine.

Find a grave with your name (that is, the name of the person who is executing the spell) or an unmarked grave. Bury the spool at the foot of the grave (bury it near the legs of the deceased), where it will be left for three days. Place the branches of wormwood on the grave at the buried man's chakra points: three branches at the top, three branches at the bottom, and the seventh in the center. Lay the offering of cookies, honey, and pennies at his feet. While at the cemetery, sew buttons on the piece of clothing. As you sew, recite:

In the green of the field, dry herbs grow. The wormwood in the meadow is as bitter as longing and dry as stone. I sew up that bitter longing and bind [name of beloved] to myself, [your name], by this tombstone. So be it!

After you finish sewing on the buttons, pour out half the bottle of wine and leave the other half at the grave. Leave a second offering of cookies, honey, and pennies at the graveyard's first crossroads. The bewitched person should wear the clothes with the buttons attached.

I advise you to use this method not only to attract someone to yourself but also when you need to get something from a person.

✳ THE LOVE SPELL

What you need: a cow's or bull's heart (depending on the gender of the bewitched), a coffin nail, two red candles, a string, a photo of the person you intend to bewitch (optional), wine, and honey.

Find the graves of a deceased husband and wife, buried side by side. Place one red candle on the wife's side and one on the husband's side. Say:

> *[Names of the deceased], I greet you. Help me in this matter of love! As you lived together all your life, so let [name] live with [name] all their life. They will be together; they cannot be without each other.*

Tie the two candles together, while saying:

> *As I bind these candles, let [names] be bound in fate. They will be together; they cannot be without each other.*

If you have a picture of the person you're enchanting, pierce it through the center with the nail. While holding the bound candles, say:

> *Let [name] be unable to eat or to sleep, to be happy or to smile without [name]. Let [name] become entranced by [name]. Let [name's] heart ache without [name]. Let [name] only see [name]. Let him/her love and think of [name], be restless without [name]. As a corpse in a coffin cannot see white light, so [name] cannot see or long for anyone but [name]. Now and forever. My word is true, my will is firm. Let it be so!*

Leave an offering of wine and honey at the graves and the crossroads.

❀ Spell during a Funeral

What you need: one red candle, wine, and sweets.

This spell uses church witchcraft (see chapter 8 for more about church sorcery). You will need to attend a funeral service at a church. Light the candle, and while the priest speaks, say very quietly, barely moving your lips:

> *Great sorrow, the weeping of generations, the tears of mothers,*
> *fathers, and young people. Young girls, old men and women, small*
> *children, all blood relatives. Go to [name], into his dreams, and*
> *torment him. Give [name] no rest or peace. Let [name] take on*
> *all the mourning for every fiber of [name]. Her/his lips, eyes,*
> *face. Transfer all the sadness and sorrow for [name] to love for*
> *[name]. As the deceased's relatives pine for him, so [name] pines*
> *for [name]. As the deceased's whole family cries and grieves for*
> *[name], so [name's] heart aches for [name]. As this candle melts,*
> *so heart of [name] will melt for love for [name]. By my word, love*
> *will not end. As it is said, so it will be.*

Recite this all while the priest speaks; keep repeating it if necessary. As soon as the priest says the last amen, say:

> *It's done forever.*

Extinguish the candle with your fingers and immediately leave the church and go to the cemetery. Put the remains of the candle on the grave of someone with the same name as the one you seek to enchant. Leave wine and sweets as an offering. As you leave the offering, say:

> *I leave this offering to you, the deceased, and I force [name] to suffer.*

❀ Spell for Suppression of the Will

What you need: a black rooster, a photo of the beloved, and vodka, pennies, cigars, or black bread.

At midnight, at the cemetery crossroads, slaughter the rooster. Use the blood of the rooster to write the name of the one you're bewitching. Recite the following spell four times in the four cardinal directions.

The devil will drain away your will, [name], as he does this blood. You won't have so much as an acre; you will be ensnared. You, [name], will be with [name]. As the devil takes this blood, so the longing for [name] will leach away your will. You'll crow like a rooster but be obediently silent before [name]. You cannot say a word against my charm. As the devil takes this blood, so will I, [name], take your love! As it spills, drop by drop, [name's] soul and body will turn to [name]. You will be enslaved to [name], now and forever. Let it be so!

Leave the rooster's carcass at the crossroads, with the photo under the rooster's remains. Leave the standard offering of vodka, pennies, cigars, or black bread. Face west as you go home.

✢ SPELL TO TORMENT SOMEONE WITH LONGING

What you need: nine needles, a cross, a black candle, personal belonging and photo of the bewitched, a cow's or bull's heart (depending on the gender of the bewitched), a black hen or rooster (again, depending on the gender), and vodka, pennies, cigars, or black bread.

This ritual is held in a cemetery at the first crossroads. Three days before you cast this spell, insert nine needles in the grave of someone with the same name as the one you seek to bewitch. On the day of the spell, retrieve the nine needles and, at the crossroads, light the candle and draw the seal of Cain (shown opposite) on the ground with dripped wax. Invert the cross and place it in the middle of the crossroads. While facing west, say nine times:

Nine forces of hell, nine demons of hell, I conjure you, I call you, with an inverted cross, spilled blood, a wax seal. On the word of a mage, I challenge you to work. To wander around the world with a human eye, a falcon's eye, a crow's wings, to find [name] and his/ her heart, and when it has dimmed, you'll strike it with arrows, enter into it, and torment [name].

You'll go where I send you. With a wax seal and an inverted cross, I conjure nine demons. I send nine forces of hell to [name's] heart, to torment him/her, burn [name] with fire, ache, and yearning, day and night to make [name] think about [name], to long for [name], cry for [name], to love [name] and only [name]; this is my hellish command. Thirteen demonic forces, I summon you to torment [name], to make [name] love [name]. Nema.

Seal of Cain

Slaughter the chicken and drip its blood over the seal of Cain, the photograph, and the personal belonging. Then take the cow's or bull's heart, put the photo on top of it, and pierce it with the nine needles while saying:

Let [name] long for [name]!
Let [name] day and night be without rest for [name]!
Let [name] yearn deeply for [name]!
Let nine demons tie [name] to [name]!
As I cry to the underworld, let [name] cry for [name]!
Let [name] boil and heat up in hell's cauldron for [name]!

> *Let [name] be exhausted for [name]!*
> *Let [name] begin to wish for [name]!*
> *Let [name] share one bed with [name]! Nema!*

Leave an offering of vodka, pennies, cigars, or black bread. This rite is strong. It takes effect quickly.

✤ SEXUAL BINDING

What you need: a red candle, a full-length photo of the beloved, a full-length photo of the woman (seeking the beloved), red thread, and honey, black bread, or wine.

This ritual is only for a woman seeking to bewitch a man and is held in a cemetery. Find a grave of someone with the same name as the person you are binding. Cut off about two inches from the bottom of the candle. Glue this piece of candle onto the genital area of the bewitched's photo. On the photo of the woman, make a hole in the genital area. Connect the two photos face-to-face, inserting the candle "penis" through the hole. Wind the thread around the "penis" as you recite nine times:

> *As I wind this thread, so I wind a noose around this penis. As I*
> *tie these knots, so I will forever tie [name] to [name]. From this*
> *hour, he will belong to [name]. His penis will stiffen for no woman*
> *except [name]. From now on, he will only want to be with [name].*
> *Let it be so!*

Tie nine knots and trim the ends of the thread. Light the candle, and as you drip the wax to seal your work, say:

> *As shadows trail after you in the dark of night, so [name] will*
> *trail after [name]. From this day on, let [name] be sad and bitter*
> *without [name]. Let [name] be unable to drink, eat, or sleep*
> *without [name]. As black cats are invisible in the black of the*
> *night, so are all other women invisible to [name]. So be it.*

Bury the photos in the grave. Make an offering of the honey, black bread, or wine.

❄ SPELL AT A CEMETERY CROSSROADS

What you need: chalk or flour, five red candles, a photograph or a personal belonging of the target, a black hen or rooster (depending on the gender of the target), and wine or honeycombs.

Conduct the ritual at midnight. Using chalk or flour, draw a pentagram at the cemetery crossroads, with the top facing the west. Light the candles and place them at the points of the pentagram, going clockwise. Place the photograph or personal belonging in the center of the pentagram. Stand in the center facing west. Turn counterclockwise and recite the following charm four times, each time facing a different cardinal direction.

I bow to the devil [bow]. I cut myself off from the cross and prayer. I spit at the Holy Trinity [spit once across your right shoulder], I stand with my back to the west. Oh, master, help me in my work. In the name of all the demons of Sodom (Baal and Molech), sear the bones and flesh of [name] with unquenchable fire, unquenchable desire for [name], so that by night and day [name] dreams of [name], so that [name's] mind is not his/her own, but all [name's] thoughts are of the lust sparked in his/her body. [Name] will forget to eat or drink and dream only about [name's] body. Love for [name] will eat at him/her from the inside. [Name's] body and mind will be aflame, and all thoughts will be of him/her.

Henceforth, there is no one who can undo this spell. No one may remove the passion from [name] toward [name], unless I do so myself. My word is strong, my will is firm. Let it be so!

Slaughter the chicken and drip its blood onto the photograph or belonging. Leave an offering, exit the pentagram, and go home. Follow all the rules.

BREAKUP AND DIVORCE SPELLS

A breakup spell or a divorce spell is aimed at destroying the energy ties between two people. Outwardly it leads to the deterioration of the couple's relationship and ends in a complete rupture. The essence of the breakup spell is to separate and alienate people who are bound by feelings of love. There are many different reasons why people use breakup spells, including unrequited love, jealousy, unwanted attention, anger, and revenge.

Most often a breakup spell is used to remove an opponent from someone's path or to separate a couple for personal reasons. You can use love breakup spells to tear an opponent away from the one you love.

✳ To Break Up a Couple

What you need: dirt from two graves with the same names as the people you want to break up, black thread, two photos (one of each person), and offerings such as honey, black bread, vodka, or wine.

After taking dirt from the two graves, leave an offering on each grave. Using black thread, sew the two photos together with their backs facing each other. Put grave dirt between the photos. As you do so, recite the following charm.

> *I call, I conjure, for [names] to break apart forever, for the world between them to stop turning, and for their relationship to grow as cold as the grave. One heart will not turn toward the other but will turn away. On the ninth day there will be a bad fight, and all love will come to an end. I pull them apart with dark words and grave dirt so that they will not be together. They will not live, love, or have children together. Amen!*

Leave the sewn-together photos at the cemetery crossroads. Don't forget the rules of work in the cemetery: you must leave offerings.

✼ A BREAKUP SPELL OVER TWO GRAVES

What you need: a bottle of wine, black bread broken in three pieces (for three separate offerings), three candles, a black piece of cloth, and a ritual knife.

You must perform the ritual under a waning moon. Go to the cemetery immediately after sunset. Find a grave with the same name as the man and another with the same name as the woman. Perform the following actions above each one.

Light a candle and say:

You, [name of the deceased], slumped over, at rest, forgive me
and help me. Let [woman's name] and [man's name] live facing
different directions, scattered forever. Let it be so.

Leave an offering (a piece of bread, pour some wine on the ground). Begin to dig up dirt from the grave with the ritual knife and recite:

I'm traveling the path of the dead. I take away [name and name's]
peace and quietness. I take away their passion. Do not let [name
and name] be together, love each other. Let it be so.

Put the dirt you have dug up in the piece of cloth.

When you stand at the second grave, repeat all the same actions you performed on the first one: ask for help from the deceased, make an offering (wine and bread), recite the spell, and dig up the dirt and put it in the cloth. Light the second candle.

Leave an offering (wine and bread) at the crossroads. Light the last candle at the crossroads. Take the dirt with you to sprinkle on the doorstep of your targets.

CURSES

A curse is the introduction of negative energy to a person through curses, spells, or special rituals.

There are several main types of curses: business failures, poor health, quarrels, separation, alcoholism, addiction, celibacy, clan or family curses, and death curses. Signs of curses include inexplicable and sharp mood swings on the part of the spouse, the presence of loose dirt or poppy seeds, sprinkled water or traces of candles, and other unusual objects in the home. Sudden weight loss for no apparent reason, unexplained irritability, sleep disturbance, frequent injuries, and illness.

A death curse is one of the strongest kinds of black magic, aimed at the magical destruction of an enemy or someone who, in the opinion of the person who seeks his death, hinders him. It is inappropriate to talk about the moral principles of a death curse or any other magical action aimed at creating problems for one's neighbor. This happens in magical practice.

A death curse is an expression of the evil, negativity, irritation, and all the negative emotions accumulated in the one who cast the death curse. But emotions and negativity alone do not create a death curse. You must perform a purposeful black magic ritual that has certain signs and consequences.

One such sign is constant bad luck, where the person keeps ending up in unpleasant situations. The person may simply be unlucky, but if the incidents end in injuries, and the person is often and unwillingly on the verge of life and death, we can assume a death curse has been cast.

Another important sign of a death curse is the spontaneous appearance of serious diseases (cancer, heart problems, strokes) that cannot be cured by modern medicine. The person starts to die before your eyes, and no one can help him.

Another sign of a death curse might be a man's apathy, his unwillingness to live or fight. He becomes indifferent to his family and job. He often wants to be left alone, thinks of death, and becomes melancholy.

❄ A FATAL CURSE

For serious curses that lead to the death of the victim, you should enter the church where the funeral service takes place. Only do this if the victim is baptized. You can light a candle for the deceased. Put it on a rectangular table in the church along with a small crucifix, and say:

God of gods, demon of demons! Let [name] be cursed for a
century, for a period of time left for him to live and is as long as a
mouse's tail! So be it!

Put the candles upside down, three in a row. You can do this at any time except during Holy Week or the Octave of Easter (the week after Easter).

Or, do the following: light the candles for health and immediately break them (carefully, so that no one would notice). Put the candle on the table, and while it burns, say:

This candle is [name of the victim]. I break it and deprive it of
happiness. So be it!

Do this for three candles in a row. There is also such a thing as a funeral candle. It's a candle that was lit and put out in a cemetery at a funeral or funeral service. Later the candle is lit from the other side and used in the necessary rituals.

❈ CURSE ON AN ENEMY'S BELONGINGS

What you need: a black candle (made in advance with grave dirt),* a bottle of vodka, a personal belonging (worn by the target of the curse), a black rooster, springwater, and black bread.

Hold the ritual at a cemetery under the full moon. Do not look for the grave in advance. At midnight, go to the first cemetery crossroads and light a candle, saying the words:

Death does not travel far from the dead. I ask the dead for help
for magical work. I travel on the path to the dead. I'll lead [name]
to death. My enemy will be entombed in the earth. He/she will

---

*When you make a candle (using beeswax; all your candles should be made of beeswax), add dirt from the graves with which you will be working.

fall to ruin, under a shroud, to dust. Be cursed to death, [name].
Forever! Amen!

At a crossroads, pour out vodka with the words:

I pour this to you, to death, to dust, for [name]!

Light the candle over the pathway to look for a grave. If it does not lead you to a grave, spit on the candle and put it out. Leave and do not look back at the cemetery. If it did lead to a grave, go to the feet of the deceased, throw the belonging at the grave, and say:

The deceased lies in the grave; his soul is asleep. I honor [name
of the deceased], and cover the living one, [name], in his shroud.*
Here you now lie; do not disturb the living. A demon led me here;
he called me to this body. I offer blood to the demon. Damn my
enemy, [name]. Forever.

As you say these words, cut off the chicken's head and pour its blood onto the grave and the personal belonging. Bury it at the foot of the grave. Give black bread and vodka as an offering. As you leave, say:

The mage made a blood sacrifice to the demon, and [name] is
bidding his life farewell. Amen.

At home, bathe yourself in springwater. Get into the tub and pour the water over yourself while saying:

Demon to demon, bring no trouble to this mage, either in body or
at home. Amen.

Pour this water out at the base of a dry stump or tree.

---

*A shroud is clothing for the deceased or a veil that covers the body in a coffin. This garment is usually white.

❈ A Curse for Serious Illness and Subsequent Death

What you need: photo of your enemy, a piece of meat, coffin nails, a piece of black cloth, unwashed piece of clothing of your enemy (optional), a candle, and offerings such as honey, black bread, vodka, or wine.

On the back of the photo, write your enemy's name seven times. Hammer the photograph of your enemy onto the meat, using the nails. Wrap the meat with the photo in a black cloth and preferably in the unwashed clothes of the enemy.

Go to the cemetery and find a freshly dug grave. Light the candle and throw the wrapped-up piece of meat on the grave. Sprinkle it with earth of the same color as the earth on the grave, saying:

I did not dress meat in clothes but dressed [name of the victim] in a shroud. As worms begin to eat this meat, so will worms start eating [name] from the inside. They will multiply, reproduce, burrow deeper into his/her bones and skin. While [name] tries to find a cure, the worms will drag him/her into the grave. So be it!

Leave an offering at the crossroads.

❈ Death Curse

This curse is intended to cause a person to commit suicide. What you need: an item of clothing belonging to your enemy, a photo of your enemy, his or her nail parings and hair, a piece of rope used to hang a man, a black candle, vodka, bread, and, if possible, a live rooster.

Make a doll out of the clothing of your enemy. Put this photo inside (with his or her name written on the back seven times), along with the nail parings and hair. Go to a cemetery exactly at midnight. Find an unmarked grave decorated with a cross. Light the candle at the feet of the deceased. Tie one end of the rope to the top of the cross while saying:

I tie a knot, I bring justice.

Then tie the other end of the rope around the doll's head, saying:

As I tie this rope, so will [name]'s bones and flesh be torn, his/her
air blocked, justice and punishment accomplished. Satan himself
will judge [name] for his/her bad deeds for his/her obsessed mind,
for his/her black soul, for his/her mortal sins. With each new day
that [name] lives, Satan will torment [name], hurt him/her, twist
him/her, will break [name's] bones and flesh. [Name's] spine will
bend. [Name's] arms will be wrenched; his/her neck will twist.
[Name] can neither inhale nor exhale. The pain will only stop
when [name] falls into the damp earth, throws his/herself into the
fire, drowns at the bottom of the river, or hangs from a rope. As I
say it, [name] will be punished. So be it!

Leave the doll to hang. Make an offering of vodka and bread at the grave and at the crossroads. If you brought a live rooster, sacrifice it at the grave and drench the doll with the blood. Leave the carcass at the grave.

❋ CLOSE THE PATHWAYS

What you need: insoles from the enemy's shoes, ribbons or ropes from the deceased,* three black candles, vodka, black bread, and raw meat.

Go to the cemetery to the grave of someone with the same name as the enemy. Face north and say to the deceased:

Greetings! You are the door! You are the open pathway.

---

*A simple and practical reason for the tied hands and feet is to keep the corpse in a funeral position, hands folded on the chest and legs lying elongated and pressed against each other. If this is not done, rigor mortis can cause the body to shift into an unappealing position. In addition, by tradition, a candle or a cross is inserted in the folded hands of the deceased. However, there is also a mystical component of this tradition that comes from paganism. According to this tradition, the ropes do not simply bind limbs but also tie the soul of the deceased to the body so that it does not remain in this world and is more easily able to travel into the otherworld. Before the burial itself, these ropes must be cut to free the soul.

Place three candles on the grave, one each at the deceased's feet, torso, and head. Stand at the deceased's feet and tie the insoles to the cross with the ropes from the deceased.

*I curse [name]; I control [name]. I ruin [name's] fate. I expel
[name] from the white light; I send [name] to the darkness. I
choose to take [name's] happiness and luck; I close all his/her
pathways, all the roads for [name], all the doors. I take [name's]
luck and success, which now belongs to me, and I leave [name]
with nothing but pain and misery. So be it!*

Bury the items in the grave with the same name as the victim. Make an offering at the grave and at the crossroads.

❊ STRONG CURSE

The mage must obtain the tibia of a hanged man.

In the Middle Ages, corpses hung on the gallows until the birds completely picked off all the flesh, and then the bones lay under the gallows. A mage could pick up the tibia and return home. There the mage put the bone on the altar and recited Our Father over it nine times, backward and in Latin.

*Nema Olam a son arebil des menoitatnet ni sacudni son en te.
Sirtson subiotibed sumittimid son te tucis, artson atibed sibon
ettimid te. Eidoh sibon ad munaiditouq murtson menap. Arreta
ni oleac ni tucis, aut satnulov taif muut munger tainevda. Muut
nemon rutecifitcnas, sileac ni se iuq retson retap.*

Then the mage appealed to the spirit of the deceased.

*Come through the noose; come over death's threshold. Let the
power of the dark release you to find your way back through the
noose. Come and do my work.*

The mage would then explain his request, usually to kill a person or a whole family. He would write his request on the bones in ink as well. After the ink was dry, he buried the bone for three days at a cemetery crossroads, saying:

Take this power through the land where Death dwells.

Three days later, the mage would return to the place where he buried the bone and dig it up. He would slaughter a black chicken and let its blood drain directly onto the bone in the hole. Then the mage would hold the bloody bone in his hands and say:

Carry this curse to those for whom I have no love.

He would bury the chicken in the same grave and leave without looking back. Usually he buried these bones near the victim's house or attempted to place it in either the foundation or the wall of the house. The people who lived in houses near the buried bones would usually begin to go crazy. Such people had the unfortunate honor of always hearing noises and seeing objects move untouched. They observed what today is called a poltergeist.

Curse to Make a Person Addicted to Alcohol

What you need: dirt from the grave of an alcoholic and from a cemetery crossroads, a jar, a photo of the victim, hair and nail parings from the victim, animal waste (dog, cat, or other animal), black pepper, cayenne pepper, and vodka.

Put the dirt from the grave (you need to know which deceased was an alcoholic when he was alive) and the crossroads in the jar. Write the victim's name on the back of the photo seven times and put it and the hair and nail parings in the jar. Add animal waste to the jar, along with generous amounts of the black and cayenne peppers and some vodka. Close the lid tightly and say:

Let [name's] life turn to shit, into a chaotic nightmare, worse than

bitter pepper. [Name's] only consolation will be bitter drunkenness,
and it will send [name] to his/her grave. So be it!

Bury this jar in the ground and plant a fast-growing species of tree over it. Call the tree by the victim's name. Water and look after the young tree. The taller and stronger it becomes, the stronger the curse will be.

✸ Death Curse

What you need: a small black candle, a photo of your enemy, hair and nail parings, an item of clothing belonging to the enemy, a string, a black rooster or hen (depending on the gender of the victim), a bottle of wine, honey, bread, and pennies.

Go to a crossroads in a cemetery. Light the candle and put it in the center of the crossroads. Tie up the enemy's photo and his or her hair and nails in the piece of clothing, and put this bundle next to the candle. Open the wine, pour it on the ground three times, and put the bottle next to the bundle. Cut off the chicken's head and let the blood flow over the bound items. As the blood drips, say:

Brothers rise, sisters rise. I will feed you with plenty. I will sate your
thirst with wine. Let this blood flow into your weak veins and fill
them with immense power. I urge you all, I conjure you all to help
me. Take [name], bury him/her. Tie [name] to your graves; torment
[name] with terrible punishments so that he/she knows the torments
of hell. Blood to blood, dust to dust, ashes to ashes. No one can
remove this, nor break this, for this is my curse. So be it!

Leave an offering (honey, bread, pennies) at the crossroads and to the mistress of the cemeteries.

✸ Serious Curse for Illness

What you need: a black rooster, a ritual knife, a piece of the victim's unwashed underwear, stiff black cotton thread, and a large needle.

At the end of the waning moon, go to the forest. Slaughter the rooster at a crossroads, using the ritual knife, and drip blood thirteen times as you say:

> *Demons of the forest, accept this offering and rot [name] from the inside. Tear [name] apart, kill [name], and lay him/her to rest in the earth. So be it!*

Cut off the feet and head of the rooster and slit open the carcass. Put the enemy's underwear inside and sew it up. Bury the rooster at the crossroads.

String up the bird's head and foot using the thread and hang them on the door handle of the victim's car or the front door of his or her home.

✿ THE GRAVESTONE

This death curse, which originated in Russia, is based on an old Russian custom of burying murderers and rapists under the coffins of their victims.

Obtain insoles from the victim's shoes (or another item of clothing) and attach them to the underside of the coffin of the deceased before the burial. Place a golden coin in the coffin of the deceased as an offering. As you do so, say:

> *As the flesh of the deceased will rot, so [name] will wither, die, and disappear. [Name's] flesh will rot in the grave, and his/her gravestone will break and crumble to the ground. Let it be so!*

After the burial, collect grave dirt and scatter it on the threshold of the victim or in the food of the victim.

✿ TO DEPRIVE AN ENEMY OF HEALTH

What you need: a well-worn and unwashed piece of clothing of the victim (T-shirt, socks, underwear), strong liquor, silver coins, tobacco or sweets, and blood sacrifice of a bird (optional).

Under a waning moon, go to a cemetery at midnight. Greet the mistress of the cemeteries with an offering of coins and liquor and ask permission to work in her domain. If at this moment, there is no strong wind or rain and you feel well, you can safely search for an active grave with the same name as the victim. The grave should be recent, no more than forty days from the moment of burial. Greet the deceased and give him or her offerings (tobacco, sweets), including, if possible, a blood sacrifice of a bird. After making the offering, bury the victim's clothing in the area of the deceased's chest. As you do so, recite the following curse.

As the body of the deceased rots and his bones dry in the earth,
so will [name's] clothing rot and dry up like a corpse in his grave.
At such a time [name], the afflicted, will die; the mistress of death
will take [name] to his/her grave. [Name] will experience three
years of great suffering. Amen!

Take a tiny pinch of dirt from the place where you buried the enemy's clothing and leave, making sure to observe the rules of cemetery magic. Add the dirt to the victim's food when the opportunity arises.

✸ DISEASE

What you need: the victim's unwashed shirt, beans, and needle and thread.

Cut the cloth out of the armpits of the shirt and sew a small pouch from the cloth. Put the beans in the pouch. Moisten the cloth with water and keep the pouch in a warm, bright place until the beans sprout. Bury the pouch shallowly in the western corner of an old cemetery. Water it periodically from a cemetery puddle (dead water) while reciting the following curse thirteen times:

As the sprout grows in [name]'s armpit, so a fierce cancer is
growing. As the sprout germinates, so it will devour [name].
[Name] will suffer pain and torment. So be it!

Once the shoot grows, harvest it, dry it, crush it into powder, and feed it to the victim.

✳ CURSE USING EGGS

Take a fresh egg from under a black hen. At midnight, three days before the rise of the waning moon, bury the egg in an active grave of someone with the same name as the victim. Make an offering to the dead. Return after three nights to present the dead with another offering. As you do so, remove the egg and recite the following thirteen times.

> *[Name] will no longer live. As [name] eats the egg, so will [name] find disease and torment and suffer and rot from the inside. [Name of the deceased] will call [name] to be buried in the earth and rest as she/he does. Amen!*

Cook the egg carefully so that it does not crack (do not use salted water) and feed it to the victim.

TRANSFERS IN MAGIC

Transfers are actions performed to pass a negative phenomena (evil eye, curses, spells, charms, diseases) afflicting someone (including yourself) to another person or animal.

✳ TRANSFERENCE OF A SERIOUS ILLNESS

If you need to revive a deathly ill person, find a target with the same name but with a different middle name. Wet a white cloth in fresh water and wipe the sick person with it. Clean his or her whole body with this cloth. Then squeeze the water into a glass while saying three times:

> *Let [name of sick person] live, and [name of enemy] die. Let [name] grow in health and strength, and let [name] wither and be destined for the graveyard. Let it be so!*

Every time you wet the cloth to clean the sick person, squeeze the water into the glass. Give your target the water to drink. Bury the cloth in a fresh grave of someone with the same name (but with a different middle name from the patient). Make a good offering and say three times:

> *Let [name of sick person] live and be healthy, let [name of enemy] stoop and ache. Let [name] lie with the dead, let [name] be called to her/his grave. Amen!*

Leave and make an offering to the mistress of the cemeteries.

✻ AN OFFERING OF A GOOSE

In the event that you made a very serious mistake in some sort of cemetery ritual, one that threatens you with death or with a severe incurable disease, you can sacrifice a goose and transfer the threat to it.

Make the offering under the waning moon. You must find the biggest Devil's Cross crossroads in a dark and deserted cemetery. Face west at the crossroads. Hold the live goose by its feet in one hand and an ax in your other hand. Recite the following four times for each direction, starting with the west, then going to the east, south, and north.

> *I came, [your name], to the bloody cross in the land of the dead.*
> *I conjure the spirits of death, spirits of misfortune, spirits of grief,*
> *spirits of failures, I call the devil's name. As you hunger for me, so*
> *do I love life. I invoke the devil's trinity [Veligor, Verzaul, or Aspid,*
> *depending on your tradition]. In the name of Satan, I conjure you*
> *to abandon me, to leave my blood, flesh, bones, guts, heart, eyes,*
> *tongue, and my immortal soul. I sacrifice this bird to you so that*
> *you may feast instead on its blood. My word is my lock; the moon*
> *is my witness. I offer this. I offer this. I offer this. Amen.*

At the fourth recitation facing north, slaughter the bird, chopping its head off. Leave it and the ax where they lay. Leave the wine as well. Bow first to the west, then to the east, then to the south, and then to the north. Leave immediately, without looking back. After this ceremony you cannot eat meat or sleep for a day.

✳ Transfer Disease at the Cemetery

What you need: a silver spoon, a cloth for wiping, three candles, black bread, nine pennies, and wine.

Before you go to the cemetery, you need to put a silver spoon under the patient's pillow for nine days. On the ninth day, wipe the patient from head to toe with it while saying (nine times):

> Let the sickness go from [name] to the silver. Take it onto yourself forever. The silver will lie with the dead and waste away as the dead do. The illness is in the silver. The illness is in the silver. And health is in [name]. So be it.

Under the waning moon, go to the cemetery and take this spoon with you. Do not touch the spoon with your bare hands. On the grave with the same name as the patient, place three candles (over the head, the legs, and the torso). Turn to the east and say:

> I bow to you [bow to the ground], [name of the deceased]. I ask in the name of my blood [if the patient is a blood relative, change the words if not], for [name], I beg! I give you silver [put the object on the ground], with the [illness]. I give it to you. Take it with you; take it to the otherworld. Take the disease from [name]; take it with you, [name of the deceased], forever and ever. The silver will lie with the dead, where the deceased rot away. The illness is in the silver and health is in [name]. So be it.

Leave an offering of pennies, wine, and bread on the grave and at the crossroads.

✳ A Rite of Wealth

What you need: ashes of the Judas tree (*Cercis siliquastrum*), a white hen, wine, three silver-colored coins, three cigars, and sweets.

Perform this ritual at a crossroads in a cemetery at midnight. Use

Seal of Asmodeus   Seal of Beelzebub   Seal of Astaroth

the ashes to draw a pentagram in the center of the crossroads, and on three sides of the pentagram draw the seals of Asmodeus, Beelzebub, and Astaroth as shown above. Tear off the hen's head while saying:

> *Asmodeus, Beelzebub, Astaroth, I call you, open the gates of darkness, give me gold and riches. Gold, pour at my feet! Gold, cling to my hands! I will know neither poverty nor misery. Let the money come to me and increase every day. Let it be so!*

Allow the blood to drip onto the three seals. Pour wine on each seal and place a silver coin on top of each one. Leave the cigars and sweets as an offering. Exit through the eastern side of the cemetery and do not turn around.

SPELLS TO CALL OR REPEL MAGES AND OTHERS

✳ A CONTRACT WITH A MAGE

What you need: vodka, a drinking glass, a cigar, one black candle, one church candle, a black hen or a rooster (depending on the gender of the person you want to make a contract with), a silver-colored coin, a black rag, a jar, a clay pot, and birch bark.

Locate the grave of a mage in advance. Under a new or full moon, enter the cemetery; do not go on a Thursday or Saturday. At the entrance or threshold of the cemetery, pour vodka and say to the mistress of the cemeteries:

Lady, grant me a visit to [the name of the mage].

Go to a crossroads in the cemetery and leave an offering. Pour a glass of vodka and place it on the right. Light the cigar and place it on top of the glass with its burning tip pointed to the east so that the smoke drifts to the east.

Go quietly to the grave. As you approach, bow at the waist and say:

I bow to you, [name of the mage]. I respect you greatly. Your deeds are black, ardent, fierce. I came to you to ask for your help, instruction, and learning. Be a mother/father to me. I am your daughter/son, dearer than relatives, closer than blood. My eyes are your eyes; my footsteps are created by you. Your thoughts are told; whispered, your spells are cast. Let [name] ask permission to link us, [your name and the name of the mage], with a contract and secure it with your word, stronger than stone.

Put the black candle and the church candle together on the grave and light them. Cut off the chicken's head and let the blood drip onto the ground in a triangular shape. Say:

I sign our contract with blood.

Put a silver-colored coin on top of the grave.

Take away a handful of grave dirt and tie it up in the black rag, knotted in the shape of a cross. In the jar, collect some water from a cemetery puddle. Go home and be as quiet as possible as you go.

At home, mix the water of the dead with one-third of the grave dirt in a clay pot. Add three drops of blood from the ring finger of your left hand. Write the name of the mage on the birch bark and place it in the pot with the water mixture. Place the knotted black rag under the head of your bed and say:

Restless spirit of [name], come and lie in my bed. Let two become one.

Sleep on your left side for the next nine nights. On the tenth night, go to the cemetery with the clay pot and pour out the water mixture where you gathered the earth. Bury the pot, with the birch bark, at the mage's feet. Cut the knot from the cloth filled with earth and place the rag and the lit black candle in the same spot at the foot of the grave.

Carry the knot with you for another nine days, tied to your belt. To cast a spell, hold the knot in your left hand and perform witchcraft over the mage's grave.

✳ To Seal a Grave against a Mage

To protect a loved one so that his grave is not used for witchcraft and his soul is not disturbed by a mage, bury a steel knife to the hilt at his grave and say:

> *Whoever begins to disturb you with witchcraft will be met with a knife. Cut, chase, tear, rend, and teach the mage a lesson. And when someone invokes you against your will, his frail body will begin to bend with deadly pain. Let it be so!*

Walk away.

✳ To Get a Debtor to Return Money

What you need: a photo of the debtor, a sheet of paper, a clay pot, five candles, five coins, a hen or rooster (depending on the gender of the target), a black ribbon, and black cloth.

Write the name of the debtor on the back of the photo. On a blank sheet, draw the seal of Mammon (shown on page 120) and write the amount that the debtor owes. Put the paper in a clay pot. Take the pot to a ravine and invoke Mammon by drawing the seal of Mammon in the dirt and placing the pot in the center of the seal. Put lit candles and five coins around the pot in five places. Ask Mammon to help repay the debt.

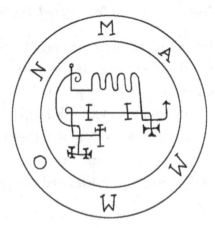

Seal of Mammon

Tie the legs of the chicken with a black ribbon and cut off its head. Let the blood drip over the burning candles and in the pot on the photo of the debtor. Announce the size of the debt to Mammon. Cut off the legs of the chicken and put them together with head in the pot. Scatter a handful of earth, taken from the ground where the seal is drawn, over the pot. Bury the chicken where the candles were burning, along with the candles and the coins. Bow and leave, taking the pot with you.

At home, pour the pot's contents onto a black cloth. Cover it with a lid and drip wax on the lid. When this is done, say:

It is so sworn.

Bury the pot in the debtor's path or at a crossroads.

❄ To Seal All Roads and Paths of Life

What you need: a black candle, vodka, an old rusty knife, blood from a black rooster, a black rag, and nine coins.

Go to a distant crossroads in a clearing where people rarely walk. Light the candle and give the offering of vodka. Dig a pit and put the knife in it. Say:

I summon the devil, bringer of strife and misfortune, from the depths
of hell. I surrender to him this rusty and deadly knife. The devil,
who wreaks destruction from the depths of the hell, will come and
take this knife and go to work against my enemies. Let him destroy
them. Let him sow discord and misfortune. Let it be so!

Drip the rooster blood into the pit with the knife and bury it. Leave
it buried for nine days. After nine days, go there at night with the black
rag. Spread it on the ground. Dig up the knife. As you unearth the
knife, say nine times:

I take this knife; I take it from the devil. I send it to my enemies.
Let the devil dwell in their deeds and their homes. Let this knife
carry my rage. Let my enemies vanish, lose their jobs, beg, starve,
and flee this place without looking back. It is so sworn!

Throw the coins in the pit and say:

Oh, Devil, I ask for your help!

Wrap the knife in the rag. Go to the house of your enemy and leave
this knife with the words:

The devil will dwell in the homes of my enemies. My enemies will
suffer, will flee this place in fear; their deeds will be overtaken by
rust. Nothing good or successful will come to them. Let it be so!

✳ To Ask for the Power of the Devil

As the moon waxes, go to the Devil's Cross (the crossroads of three
roads) in the wilderness and light a black candle made by hand from
wax and soot with a small amount of blood from your left hand, in its
center. Recite the following words nine times.

I summon thee, Devil, and pray to you. I praise you, honor you,
and acknowledge you on the way to your abode. At this very

*moment my mind is merging with yours, and I am being filled with
your strength. By this power it is done on Earth and will soon
be done again in heaven. Your power will reign in heaven as your
power contains the pure truth of the universe.*

After you finish, leave the candle there and walk away without looking back. This method can help if rituals do not work, lack strength, or
are weakened.

8
PRINCIPLES OF
CHURCH SORCERY

Followers of black magic go to church for the following purposes:

- to cure a disease
- to transfer or cast a curse
- to rejuvenate
- to curse a wedding
- to curse someone's fate
- to lead an enemy to death

Whatever goal they pursue, black mages widely practice black magic in a church. The strongest curses are cast in churches. As a rule, while the victim is standing and praying, the mage approaches him, breathes lightly into his ear, and then says the spell. A short while later, the person starts to gasp for breath. He begins to suffer from severe asthma and eventually dies of suffocation. The power and capabilities of black magic are unimaginable. In most cases, such rituals are conducted by black mages or mages who work very closely with demons.

Church sorcery is performed under the church's roof. In most cases this magic involves the twelve infernal spells (see section in chapter 9,

"The Twelve Infernal Spells of Heretics or Veretnics") or a curse on the day of a funeral.

Professional black mages always visit churches shortly before they close. At such times, parishioners are practically absent, and no one will pay special attention to the black practitioner. During this period blasphemers typically

- turn a church candle upside down or break it in several places before lighting it (depending on what a mage intends to do)
- spit on icons (to make demons work faster)
- snuff out other people's candles (if someone lit a candle to pray for peace, cure a sick person, etc., snuffing out such a candle gives a mage energy)
- steal still-burning candles while reading the black psalter (these candles can be used for inflicting a fatal disease)

This same time is used by black mages to recite demonic prayers with the aim to confuse a priest's mind or hide a required item behind a necessary icon.

The black practitioner also chooses sunset (afternoon mass) because it is when the church demon, Abar, is most powerful. The deeper the night is, the stronger he becomes. For church black magic rituals, you should not choose a Sunday during daylight. There is a huge crowd of people at the church, and it is almost impossible do anything without to being seen. The goal is to hide pictures behind church icons on the eve of a funeral feast or to invert candles. Very often on such days, there is a strong resistance to this kind of black activity. In addition to the sensations and impossibility of secret rituals on Sundays, demons do not want to come into contact with the church on this day because of its constant flow of prayers.

On Sunday, a black mage comes to the church solely for one purpose: to order a memorial or a service to commemorate a victim (as if he were dead) or to break up a loving couple. All these steps are taken to weaken the victim. If you first take away a person's energy, he can get sick more easily, or if magic is performed after weakening the victim, the spell will manifest more quickly and powerfully. Reciting church prayers backward is an excellent way to nurture demonic energy. Blasphemy on religious holidays also has great value. It is on such days that curses or spells have a special power. They can be performed not only on the altar of a black mage but also directly in the church itself, even during the service.

The black mage has never been a friend to the church, but nevertheless, he needs it to accomplish his black deeds. That is why professional black mages always put extra effort into casting curses on Easter. It is almost impossible to remove these curses. The peak of black witchcraft is a ritual aimed at defilement of the church. Such rituals are held to redirect energy flows so that, while saying their prayers, all parishioners are giving their energy not to the white forces but to feed the demon Abar and his demonic church assistants. Because doing this is a very large and unforgivable sin by Christian standards, this act is capable of giving a mage great power.

There are a great number of black magic rituals associated with churches. Mages practice rituals at crossroads near churches, at church doors, or before the church gates. In the chronicles of black magic, it is written that every time a black mage enters church premises, he gives praise to the demon Abar, thereby glorifying him. Doing so helps to draw closer the arrival of the Antichrist and the time when all mages will be reborn as half demons and rule Earth together with their master, Lucifer.

MAGE BEHAVIOR IN THE CHURCH

Today black magic performed in the church is done according to a strict code or set of rules that cannot be violated if you want to achieve a positive and expected result from the ritual. In a church, a black mage must do certain things to protect himself from other mages and must not make mistakes.

- The mage must not allow someone else to light another candle from his candle. This rule especially applies if the person seeking to light his candle is, himself, a black practitioner. Politely offer matches, which are often available in churches, or suggest another source of fire, such as the candelabra itself.

- If a black mage purchased a cross or icon for specific rituals, under no circumstances should they be given away to others.

- It is forbidden under pain of death for a mage to help place a candle in a candelabra, even if an extremely weak person asks.

- No matter how tempting it is, a mage cannot pick up any object lying in the churchyard. One way or another, it will become part of a curse or other black rite.

- A black mage is forbidden to listen to the advice of others in the church concerning what to do and how and where. In such cases, the mage may become an unwitting participant in another's black church rite.

- The rituals of black magic held in the church prohibit a black mage from listening to others, let alone fulfilling the requests of other people. A black practitioner should be especially wary of an unclear request from people the mage doesn't know.

- It is strictly forbidden to bring icons, candles, or candies at the request of others. Everyone is capable of independently buying everything they need. Such services often end with cursing or other evil. Although it is not advisable, friends and family can be the exception to this rule.

- It is strictly forbidden for mages to accept anything from other people in a church, even innocuous objects, such as handbags, icons, or crosses. All these objects can become elements of a secret black ritual.

- Before the mage exits the church, he or she must whisper these words: "I entered clean, and clean I will leave."

In addition to the aforementioned rules of behavior, a black mage must also know how to use church candles.

- Soft wax candles are used to influence an enemy.
- Candles are placed upside down to weaken the will of the enemy, destroy his astral immunity, or for more extreme influence.
- Broken or gnawed candles are used to curse or weaken the protection of the mage's victim.
- Per funeral custom, candles are placed at the entrance of where the funeral is held on the eve of the ritual to weaken or take away health.
- To cast a light curse, have memorial candles delivered to a living enemy.*
- Use memorial candles to weaken the will of the victim or his resistance to the mage's ritual.

The mage should look for signs and be wary of possible black magic competitors in the church. Indications that another practitioner is working against the mage include someone

- lighting a candle from the mage's candle
- placing another candle over the mage's candle
- rapidly snuffing out the mage's candle
- rearranging both the lighted and the extinguished candles
- removing the mage's lit candle before it has completely burned away

It's especially important to make certain, while conducting the church ritual, that the placed lit candle completely burns away. The mage should not allow a sexton or novice sister to take away an unburned candle. This "disgrace" cannot be tolerated.

---

*Candles in the Orthodox church are kept in two boxes in the narthex—one for the living and one for the dead (memorial candles). The memorial candles can be used on the living as a curse.

9

CHURCH SPELLS

EASTER CURSES

The suitable times for casting curses during Easter include the following:

- the night between Saturday and Sunday
- from Sunday sunrise to sunrise on Monday
- during Easter services

✱ EASTER CURSE FOR A PAINFUL DEATH

The proposed rite will cause the victim to die a long and extremely painful death. The essence of the ritual is to find the thinnest church candle and break it nine times. With each break the mage says:

Wither! Rot! Die!

The words need to be pronounced quietly. Then the black mage lights the candle on both sides and immediately connects both sides, linking the ends together (making a perfect round) and sealing in the burning wicks. With this action, he pronounces another spell.

I seal the life of [name].

Next, he immediately throws the candle on the memorial table, without delay. After casting the curse, the black mage immediately

128

leaves without looking back. At midnight he goes to a crossroads with a traditional offering of pennies and rum.

In black rituals, the church and magic are one. It is the powerful energy that gathers under the church domes that can satisfy the insatiable hunger of otherworldly demons. In turn, as a token of gratitude, they are always ready to respond to the call of a mage and help him in his planned atrocities. The next ritual, which is often used in Easter black practice, is the so-called white curse.

❀ THE WHITE CURSE RITUAL

The result of such a curse is terrible. It causes a serious illness of internal organs, which seem to rot under the skin, and leads to death. For this ritual, the mage uses a chicken egg, wrapped for some time in onion peels. At Easter, he takes this egg to be blessed. It is strictly forbidden to carry other components of the Easter basket. On the same day he carries the conse-crated egg to the cemetery and buries it in the grave of someone with the same name as the victim. It must remain buried in the grave dirt for exactly twenty-four hours. He buries the egg while saying the following spell.

> *I seek no forgiveness for sins I have committed, nor redemption.*
> *I am turning the Easter egg into a coffin, and therefore the living*
> *into the dead. As [name of the deceased] lies in his/her grave, so*
> *does [name] eat the egg and find him/herself in the coffin. I do not*
> *believe in the father, nor in his son, nor in the holy spirit. I serve*
> *demons in faith, with loyal service. My word is strong. So be it!*

On Monday morning the mage digs the egg out of the grave. He should feed it to his victim on the same day.

❀ FORTY DAYS' PRAYER FOR THE DEAD

A forty days' prayer is a special type of prayer that is performed daily according to the church customs for forty days after person's death.

Black practitioners order the forty days' prayer for a living person to weaken his will and defense before committing any ritual. The prayer is also intended to weaken the possibility of a successful attempt at removing a curse, spell, or other witchcraft.

It is worth remembering that in most churches, priests require someone requesting a forty days' prayer service to present a photocopy of a death certificate. A mage can use a gaunt face and completely black clothing to help circumvent this law. Naturally we are not talking about a black robe but about a mourning suit. In other cases, you may need a special piece of paper with a golden cross on it.

DAILY BLACK RITUALS

Old black magic rituals, which are conducted by black mages in churches, are diverse. It is impossible to list them all, much less describe them. Therefore, just a few are described below.

✵ THE TRANSFER OF A CURSE OR ILLNESS

What you need: three black candles, one photo of a recently deceased person, one photo of the ill or cursed living person, a knife, a stone the size of a chicken egg taken from a cemetery (leave a nickel in its place), twelve coins, wine, and black bread.

First go to church and attend the funeral service for the person to whom you will make the transfer. Do it on any day in the evening. Light the candles. Put the two pictures on the memorial table. Place a knife to the left of the photos. On the right, place the stone. Look at the photo of the deceased and say nine times:

> *My power and kingdom, forever and ever. My power is from the*
> *very beginning of time. From a black book, in a secret book. It*
> *is written in my blood, and so I was destined: The power that*
> *will be given is evil. The good will go from one to the other. The*

*blasphemy of human souls, endowed with a curse. Let it change
places. So it is sworn. Amen.*

Take the knife and put the tip over the flame of the candle for some
time, until it is covered with soot. Touch the knife to the photo of the
ill or cursed person, trace it counterclockwise against the photo, and say
the following words nine times.

*What is done, is done in word, is done in grave land, in a
whispering witch's eye. A mage's glance is thrown at you, [name
of the cursed], the needle that pierces, the fire that burns. As it
is sung in church, so I take it from you. I do not drive it away but
impart it to [name of the deceased's] body. Amen.*

Place that photo face-to-face with the photo of the deceased person
to whom you are making the transfer. Say these words nine times:

*Let it separate from the body, soul, and spirit of [name] and seek
a new home. It is impossible not to walk in the ways of the secret
blasphemy, not to seek new places, not to think, not to yearn. Shoot
the black arrow from the body, soul, and spirit of [name] into the
body, soul, and spirit of [name], there to find a new home. Live,
curse, in the body of [name]. Sound, in a mage's words, in the ears
of [name]. Go into the grave of [name], not [name]. Amen.*

As you put the stone on top of the photo of the deceased, say the
following words nine times.

*The stone is heavy; the blasphemy is strong; the curse is true.
With this stone, I press down the blasphemy, the curse, all that
hell has granted. Shift from [name] to [name], never to return.
There is no way back; there is no other way. Amen.*

Put a candle next to the stone. Let the candle burn completely. Keep
the photos for nine days. Then take them apart and take the photo of

the one to whom the transfer was made to the crossroads with the stone and an offering of coins, wine, and bread.

✤ RITUAL FOR REMOVING SICKNESS IN THE CHURCH

In a black mage's life, anything can happen, and therefore he must be always ready for anything. People get sick, but not everyone is given the opportunity to give their illness to someone else, as if they were wearing clothes. However, with the help of black magic, this is an option; it can be done.

If the illness has exhausted the black mage's body, then it can be conveyed in a very simple way: go to the door handle of the church and hold it for a while. Whisper:

> *I open the door; I drive the illness away. Whoever follows me will take it on himself.*

After pronouncing such words, you cannot immediately enter the premises of the church. It is necessary to step back a little and look at who will grab the handle and open the door to the church. As soon as the victim enters the church, the mage must say the following spell.

> *The door of the church is opened, my purpose is arranged, in the church he will pray, but he will walk away with my pain.*

If the disease is serious, then this ritual must be carried out over the door handle of the church at least three times.

Mages use parishioners as carriers of their grievous fates, various diseases, or curses. Another ritual will tell you how else you can give a person in church a mage-tormenting disease.

✤ LOVE SPELL IN CHURCH

A love spell cast in a church is the strongest one that exists. It is extremely stable and gives the black practitioner unprecedented control over his victim. Nevertheless, do not forget that the side effect after its execution is incredibly strong and it can harm the customer. Love spells that occur within church walls are always made on the waxing moon.

Before you enter the church, you need to cross yourself, but do so as if turning away from the cross and bow. In the church, buy the largest candle. Pay more than necessary, but do not take the change; leave it for the church. Next, turn to face the altar and do the same as the others: bow or kneel and pretend to listen and pray.

After some time, the black practitioner should approach the place where the icons are collected and find the icon of the Blessed Virgin. Opposite her, light a candle. After that, return again to the altar and recite the following spell to yourself from memory.

The house of God, the threshold of God, the throne of God. Love power and mighty, but raging tears of jealousy. Send suffering through each and every part of [name of male victim], on his head and his temple, in his heart and liver, his veins and blood, in all his joints. In each thought, with each yelp and sigh, in his heart and mind. Let him not sleep or eat. Let him be trapped. There are ten winds, and the tenth is a whirlwind. Grip his mind so that he cannot eat, nor lie, nor sit. Everything is torn away from him to be given to [name of female client]. Everything leaves him. He hears the mage's voice everywhere. He cannot breathe fresh air. Like a fish on the shore with no water, [name] will wither without [name of client]; like grass without mother earth, [name of victim] will die away. As there is no sky without clouds, so [name of victim] will never approach anyone. My words are strong and firm. Amen.

THE TWELVE INFERNAL SPELLS OF HERETICS OR VERETNICS

✤ THE FIRST INFERNAL SPELL

To send an enemy's spirit into the realm of the dead to disappear forever, at Christmas obtain a lock of hair or an undergarment from the enemy, as well as a nail and an ax. Take them, buy offerings, and go to the graveyard. The mistress of glory and goodness will let you find the right grave. Once you find it, fasten the lock of hair to the center of the cross with the nail, and say thirteen times:

> *Not in the name of the father, the son, or the Holy Spirit, but in the name of the forces of the damned, who will rise from hell and have total power on Earth and in heaven. As Jesus was hung from the cross in excruciating pain and with a withering body, so release [name's] spirit to enter the realm of the dead. Let it disappear and not be resurrected as Jesus was. Nema! Nema! Nema!*

And then leave as befits a Veretnic.

✸ The Second Infernal Spell

To send an enemy to his grave, go to the church during the Epiphany. Place a candle inside the church, break the candle in the middle, and say thirteen times, quietly:

> *Not in the name of the father, the son, or the Holy Spirit, but in the name of the forces of the damned, I come here before you, the forces of the damned, as you rise to heaven. Everyone will bow before you. Now, I ask for aid. As I blasphemously broke the candle, so let the power of the curse break [name] and send [name] to his/her grave. Nema! Nema! Nema!*

✸ The Third Infernal Spell

To drive an enemy out of his house and onto the streets to starve, during the winter solstice, take a piece of fur from a stray dog. On the night before people go caroling, turn a church candle upside down and drip wax onto the fur. As you do so, say the following spell thirteen times.

> *Not in the name of the father, the son, or the Holy Spirit, but in the name of the forces of the damned, I am (your name),*

a Veretnic or heretic, and I ask that [name], like a stray dog,
starves, thirsts, and has no place to live. Let [name] be chased
to his/her home, that the wicked demon may drive [name] into
poverty and ignominy. Nema! Nema! Nema!

After saying the spell, roll the fur and wax into a ball and leave it at
your enemy's home.

❉ THE FOURTH INFERNAL SPELL

To invite a demon to live in the house of your enemy, on Palm Sunday,
go to a church and take a small amount of wax from a memorial candle. Roll the wax into a ball and let it roll into the dusty corners of
the church. (Not a lot of corners, just as many as you can easily find.)
Whisper the following thirteen times.

Not in the name of the father, the son, or the Holy Spirit, but
in the name of the forces of the damned, I bow my head to you
and ask that, as the hated Jesus Christ passed into Jerusalem
on this day in ages gone, so let the prodigal wicked demon enter
into [name's] house on this day. The master will begin to live in
[name's] house. He will destroy and ruin everything within, and the
people who live there will neither sleep nor drink nor eat nor earn.
Their light and life will dim and fade. Nema! Nema! Nema!

Take this ball of wax and dust to the home of your enemy and leave
it there.

❉ THE FIFTH INFERNAL SPELL

To wish destruction upon an enemy, on Easter, walk around the church
as in the procession, holding an Easter cake in your hands. Quietly say the
following spell thirteen times under your breath while looking at the cake.

Not in the name of the father, the son, or the Holy Spirit, but
in the name of the forces of the damned, let the wicked forces

ascend to heaven and rebel for all eternity. I ask that you fell and
vanquish my foes, that you, wicked forces of the damned, take
away [name's] mind and memory, rot [name's] heart and liver,
ravage and rip away [name's] flesh, crush [name's] gravestone into
dust. Nema! Nema! Nema!

In the morning, give this cake to your enemy.

❀ THE SIXTH INFERNAL SPELL

If you want to deprive a pregnant woman of her fetus, on the night
before the Annunciation, take a fresh egg that has turned gray from
beneath a chicken. The egg represents embryo; not an egg from Walmart
but an egg from a farmyard. This is old-world witchcraft. The egg is the
birth of a new life, a representation of the sun, child, and embryo. At
midnight, go to the home of the woman, smash the egg on her doorstep,
and recite the following thirteen times.

Not in the name of the father, the son, or the Holy Spirit, but in
the name of the forces of the damned, the forces now ascend to
the heavenly kingdom to reign over all on Earth and in heaven. I
ask these forces, as I destroy this egg and kill God's offspring, so
let [name] be deprived of her offspring, and the child within her be
killed. Nema! Nema! Nema!

❀ THE SEVENTH INFERNAL SPELL

Use this spell to send death to an enemy. On the eve of the Ascension,
take an icon with the same name as your enemy to the cemetery. Go to
the grave of someone with that name and bury the icon at the head of the
grave along with a generous offering. Recite the following thirteen times.

Not in the name of the father, the son, or the Holy Spirit, but in
the name of the forces of the damned, I cast this spell on [name],
the dead. As the hated Jesus ascended to heaven on this day, so let

[name] go to this grave, that [name's] soul may be rendered to the forces of damned. Nema! Nema! Nema!

✣ THE EIGHTH INFERNAL SPELL

To break up an enemy's home, from morning until evening on Pentecost slowly chew roasted sunflower seeds, one by one, and spit each one out. At the same time, quietly say the following for each seed you chew.

Not in the name of the father, the son, or the Holy Spirit, but in the name of the forces of the damned, as the Holy Spirit this day and this night descended from heaven, so the wicked forces are now ascending from hell to the kingdom of heaven to begin their reign. I ask these forces, as these shells are empty, so let the home of [name] be empty and broken forever. Nema! Nema! Nema!

Discard the shells on the enemy's doorstep at midnight.

✣ THE NINTH INFERNAL SPELL

During the Assumption, go to the church and place a candle for the enemy's peaceful rest, praying the following thirteen times.

Not in the name of the father, the son, or the Holy Spirit, but in the name of the forces of the damned, I invoke the forces before me: as Mary the wretch died on this day, so let [name] die, decay, wither, rot, and go to [name's] place in the earth. Nema! Nema! Nema!

✣ THE TENTH INFERNAL SPELL

To bring poverty, hunger, and ruin to a person or family by disrupting the harvest, use this spell. On the night of Kupala, take a pot of dead water from the cemetery and weave a wreath of flowers from the cemetery.

Wet the wreath in the dead water, and splash the water on the livestock you want to sicken and strike dead. Sprinkle the water over the gardens and fields and say:

*Not in the name of the father, the son, or the Holy Spirit, but in
the name of the forces of the damned, let the force do as I ask
and render the land barren. Let the harvest not be reaped, let the
livestock not be fed, let the goods not be stored, let the ears in
the fields not be picked, and let the products of the livestock not
be gathered. Let everything be overgrown and strangled by weeds.
Nema! Nema! Nema!*

⁂ THE ELEVENTH INFERNAL SPELL

To imbue water with death, recite the following spell thirteen times
over a bowl of water.

*Not in the name of the father, the son, or the Holy Spirit, but in
the name of the forces of the damned, I bow to them. As on this
day the resurrected Jesus appeared to the women, so will they
appear to [name] and drive [name] from his/her senses. Nema!
Nema! Nema!*

Serve this water to the enemy.

⁂ THE TWELFTH INFERNAL SPELL

At midnight, before the feast of the Intercession of the Holy Virgin,
take an armful of dry weeds and burn them into ash. Cast the ashes on
the land of the one who displeases you. Say the following thirteen times
and then leave.

*Not in the name of the father, the son, or the Holy Spirit, but in
the name of the forces of the damned, I bow before them. This
is the moment when Mary the wretch birthed her child. As the
people of Constantinople salted the earth so that not a grain would
grow, so let nothing grow here. Nema! Nema! Nema!*

10

BLOOD MAGIC

Blood is a special substance for a black mage. The blood in our veins pulsates and flows. It spreads nutrients throughout the body and also helps cleanse impurities. Only blood can regenerate.

Blood in black magic is identified with the soul of a person, his life stream, and his astral energy. Among all the components used in black magic, blood has been and continues to hold the leading position in terms of strength and frequency of use. Since time immemorial, there have been a tremendous variety of ways to perform dark rituals with blood. The magic of voodoo gives blood a special role in its rituals.

In practice, the strength of blood is insurmountable. Divination and spells become especially effective weapons or instruments when conducted with the help of blood. Sexual spells have become more popular in recent years, and blood can triple their impact.

The energy and strength in blood can establish a direct connection with the forces of darkness. It was blood magic that allowed black mages to find their most powerful patron: Lucifer. When the mage gave his soul to the Lord of Darkness, he signed the contract with his own blood, not with ink.

Over time, black magic rituals were perfected, and instead of blood, black mages began using various red items instead, such as red wine, gems (rubies, garnets), paper, fabric, containers, and symbols. Still, the most powerful rituals in black magic are those that are carried out by mages using the blood of sacrificial birds or animals.

Love spells are one of the many rituals in which using blood is important. Ancient black blood magic can offer an uncountable number of ritual variations of this dark witchcraft. If a black mage is a woman or is required to bewitch a man, then menstrual blood is used. But always keep in mind that menstrual blood is considered dead, rotten blood: it will bind the man to the woman, but it will make him violent toward the woman or make him addicted to alcohol. He may cheat on the woman all the time and try to hide it, but he will not be able to leave the woman. If you want to use blood, better to use blood from a finger. If the practitioner is a man or the practitioner's customer is male, blood is obtained from any finger of the left hand.

Concerning the use of ritual blood in love spells, several steps and guidelines must be followed. The most significant or important of these are counting the number of blood drops, using required whispers or spells, and the precise use of food or drink.

Experienced mages suggest adding blood to red wine or another, dark-colored alcoholic beverage. If you are adding it to meat, it is best added to rabbit or pigeon, which is then dried in the oven or with other heat. The use of blood in magic not only bewitches an object of desire but also makes him submit fully to the customer or the practitioner.

Black spells on blood are used, as a rule, when other methods have already been tried and the final result has not been achieved. If the spell has worked, but the victim is no longer desirable, it is best to remove the spell and release the person. Otherwise the practitioner can be overtaken by an energy similar to a backlash or an energy strike.

Love spells on the blood are quite diverse in the ways they are cast.

✳ LOVE SPELL USING BLOOD

Add a few drops of blood to a man's red wine while saying the following words.

As I cannot be without blood, so [name] cannot be without me.

Use blood from a ring finger located on the left hand. The number of drops required is also an odd number. As the drops of blood drip into the wine, you need to say the following words.

As soon as you, [name], drink my blood, with the magic wine you swallow, you will rush to me with mad passion. All thoughts, desires, everything will only be mine and only about me.

✤ PREPARING A POWERFUL LOVE POWDER

On Friday, the witch spills her blood long after midnight. In this case menstrual blood is ideal, but it should be collected right at the beginning of the menstrual cycle, on day one. She pours it into a clay pot. Then she adds a rabbit or pigeon heart to it. She dries all the contents under the sun for several days until it becomes a fine powder. She gives this powder to the object of her desire.

✤ BLOOD CURSE POWDER

To drive an enemy into the grave, the black mage uses the heart of a sparrow, a dove, or a swallow. He dries it with the blood of the victim. He grinds this mixture to a fine powder and carries it with him for the required time.

✤ BLOOD LOVE SPELL ON APPLES

Just before sunrise, harvest one of the most beautiful apples in the garden, but only on a Friday. Write down your name with your own blood on a small piece of paper, as well as the name of the person you want to bind. Fold it and wrap it in three hairs each from the object of your desire and from you. Cut the apple into two halves, and remove the core from each half. Put the scrap of paper with the names in the groove, and bind the halves together with a myrtle twig. Wrap the apple in laurel leaves, and place it under the pillow of the person you want to bewitch.

METHODS FOR OBTAINING RITUAL BLOOD

All magic, including voodoo, uses blood in its rituals. However, the use of blood itself does not guarantee success in carrying out the ritual because the black magic of the spell said during the ritual is also needed. If blood is used and the ritual is carefully performed, all the conditions will have been met to fulfill the spell. However, one more step is necessary before the ritual can be successfully carried out, and that is correctly obtaining blood.

In black magic, there are several ways to properly take blood, which will guarantee more than 70 percent success in the ritual. It is necessary to know the correct day, time, and way to collect it. Blood can be obtained from a wound that is inflicted on the victim. In this case, it is ready for use in rituals of consecration, in military magic, as the food for the powers of darkness, and as a sacrifice. Blood can also serve as the most powerful source of strength for a black mage.

One of the other ways of getting blood is purely feminine: menstrual blood. This blood has simply unimaginable energy. It is used in rituals of love magic, but it can also be used to destroy or curse a person.

Blood obtained in different ways provides an opportunity not only to influence the person but also to conduct rituals to connect with wildlife in particular, especially to trees that contribute to the black mage's rituals. Very often in black magic, mages fill amulets and staffs (warlock sticks or crooks) with blood because it is such a powerful energy source. Every black action has its price, however. There are rituals in which trees are paid in blood for helping in rituals by providing their wood for a staff. Some types of staffs can only work when the wood comes from trees in a nearby forest.

Using blood in black magic rituals is powerful, and the mage must consider sincerely and without self-deception if he can handle the ritual. As already mentioned, any magical action in which the forces of darkness take part is a powerful instrument, and they do not wait long for payment. The black mage should only engage in actions for which he knows he can pay.

11

PACT WITH THE DEVIL

The history of the relationship between man and the devil is a very old one. Regardless of their religion and caste, people tried from time to time to get closer to the Prince of Darkness. Some needed his strength to achieve political power, others sought to learn the unknown, some wanted money, still others, love. In short, these are the typical things that mortals want from the devil.

And what could they offer in return? Their souls. But alas, not every soul is a commodity. The Prince of Darkness is not interested in everyone. Not every mage can get in direct contact with him. The devil chooses only those who are worthy, only those who have made something of themselves and have proved it in practice. If the devil deems the petitioner unworthy, his attempts can end in failure and even death.

Pacts with the devil have played out frequently in fiction. It is enough to mention the legendary Faust of Goethe. This classic work is based on various medieval legends and tales of a real man, alchemist and mage Johannes Faust. Many legendary or semilegendary personalities were attributed to Beelzebub. The greatest violinist of all time, Nikolo Paganini, was buried without last rites or forgiveness of his sins. Why? Unholy magic or the devil (according to eyewitnesses) helped the musician during his concerts. Some particularly sensitive people directly pointed out that during the performances they personally saw the Horned One.

Indeed, the musical career of this violinist, who could play even on one string, cannot help but astonish the imagination. Another very notable and legendary figure is the famous Count Phoenix or Count Cagliostro, who is popular with writers. Many people paid tribute to this man in their works. But besides his purely scandalous glory, Cagliostro was the cleverest and most educated man of his time. He was interested in alchemy, medicine, and other natural and exact sciences.

During the Renaissance, the minds and hearts of so many people were shocked by the deeds of Cornelius Agrippa. Despite the fact that this gentleman had no degree, he is known today because of his fundamental work in occult practices. Among other things, Agrippa became famous as a mage and an alchemist, which was enough for him to be accused of mortal sin, imprisoned, and sentenced to death. However, he managed to escape and die free.

It is not without reason that it is believed that Agrippa's knowledge was received from the devil in exchange for his immortal soul. Ironically, however, the majority of church leaders were in collusion with the devil. The first documented case of a deal struck with Beelzebub is, paradoxically, that of a Christian priest from Cilicia, St. Theophilus. Such legends, for obvious reasons, are considered to be apocrypha by the church. However, it is surprising in this story that the holy father formed a contract with the devil himself to gain an ecclesiastical position in the church! Later even Roman popes were suspected, with a greater or lesser degree of proof, of transactions with the Prince of Darkness.

Consider, for example, Pope Sylvester II, who wrote works on mathematics, invented the pendulum, and introduced Arabic numerals. He also became famous as a reformer of the Catholic Church. It is possible that Sylvester II was accused of consorting with the devil because he maintained good relationships with outstanding scientists and thinkers of Arabia who, according to the regressive attitude of the Catholic Church, were considered unholy and demonic. However, one cannot help but be amazed that Sylvester II behaved somewhat strangely for a Catholic priest and was interested in things that the majority of the backward and degenerate holy fathers had not the slightest interest in or knowledge of. Furthermore, he could not come up with an excuse for his behavior.

In the modern era, many contemporary representatives of culture and art have been accused of dealing with the devil, among them the legendary Beatles. One member of the group at one time reasonably noted that the Beatles were more popular than Christ. What accounted for the sudden and sharp rise of an average English rock group to the very top of the musical Mt. Olympus? Some members of the group pointed directly and indirectly to help from higher powers, for which they all had to pay in due time.

Although many skeptics doubt the possibility of forming such a contract, the facts revealed in the twentieth century point directly to the opposite. Documents found in Germany after the end of World War II included an astounding contract signed by Hitler himself back in 1932. In this document, the Führer gave his soul in return for unlimited power over the German people. The term of the contract was exactly thirteen years, after which the soul of the "leader of all the Aryans" would be at the disposal of the devil. A careful handwriting analysis confirmed the authenticity of the Führer's signature. This contract would explain the otherwise inexplicable rise and exaltation of a half-educated corporal. There were much more worthy candidates for the post of leader among the other members of the National Socialist Party, who were much more creative and intellectual ("Hitler's Pact with the Devil Was Real," Yoga Esoteric website, posted March 2015).

The deal with the devil is the most important step in the life of every nontraditionalist. It is comparable to birth, and in fact it is a form of birth. After all, after the conclusion of the corresponding contract, the old person disappears, and a new one is in his place. It does not matter that this person has the same name, body, and habits.

Before you appeal to the Prince of Darkness, you must decide what exactly you want from him. Satan does not like it when desires change like the weather, or when some very clever mage is trying to bargain for a profit. In addition, mages must have a solid track record in order to appeal to him. In turn, a person who has decided on such a desperate act must absolutely trust his master, the devil, and believe in his all-encompassing power and might.

Often, in various magical or pseudomagical sources, one can find descriptions that say it is enough to clearly formulate your petition, and then the devil's henchmen will appear before this person, ready to conclude a contract at that very hour. It is impossible to imagine a more harmful delusion. Yes, there are a lot of rites for calling Satan and making contracts with him. Some have been passed down from previous generations; others have been borrowed from older cultures. Of course you can try to organize and hold a rite, but having no magical experience behind them and not being famous for anything in this field, only a foolish neophyte will be sure of a positive result.

A contract with the devil is considered indestructible. You should not even try to outwit the Prince of Darkness and look for loopholes so as to avoid fulfillment of certain conditions. The dark forces never forgive someone who reneges. The retribution will be swift and very cruel. Various Christian legends of people who made an agreement with the devil and then successfully deceived him and set out on the path of righteousness are completely worthless. The priests of the church were merely trying to maintain their influence over the flock. In practice, not one person, not even the most experienced mage, has succeeded in outwitting Satan.

An experienced mage of the highest category always carries out this kind of deal in the strictest secrecy and in complete solitude. As a rule, a mage does not require bags of gold for himself or the love of all women and men. By signing such a contract, higher mages seek to acquire something completely different. They need certain knowledge and skills that are simply unattainable otherwise. After all, they work with the subtlest material. Such mages need truth and knowledge in their purest form, and of course they would never exchange them for trifles.

The contract must be written (or at least signed) in blood. Historically the contract was written in Latin, but that is more a tribute to tradition than a strict necessity. It can even be written in a native dialect. The main requirement is blood. Without it, the contract will go nowhere.

Whatever dialect it is written in, there must be no equivocation, no complex turns of language or other legal tricks. All details should be clearly stated. If you miss something, you can only blame yourself. Hemming and hawing is not tolerated.

If the demon has responded to your request, then you will immediately feel it. Everyone feels him in his or her own way. After the demon's appearance, the contract should be said loud and clear, without pause. After a thorough reading, you can then sign the contract. For these purposes, make an incision on your left wrist, dip a special ritual quill in your own blood, and write your signature. Next you must burn the contract on the fire of the same candle used to draw the sigils (symbols with magical power).

Rites of this kind indicate that the paper should catch fire immediately. This is a sure sign that the devil responded positively to your request. The ashes should be carefully collected down to the smallest specks and stored in a secret place, at least until the contract ends. If the ashes are lost, then your days are numbered. Also, such black magic rituals require a clear internal organization and unconditional confidence in the correctness of such a step. Any emotional hesitation can be regarded as disrespect or fear. The devil's retribution is swift. There have been cases when mages were simply torn to pieces during the rite due to their hesitation, and some did live to see the morning.

In general, such rituals must be preceded by a whole series of preparatory actions. As a rule, rituals for establishing communication with the dark forces are preceded by a strict nine-day fast and complete abstinence from alcohol, tobacco, or other carnal pleasures for the same period.

The crossroads of abandoned roads, which are one of the most popular places for carrying out various kinds of magical rites and rituals, are also suitable for making a deal with the devil. Some sources recommend that you go to the chosen crossroads before sunrise on a Sunday morning. There, repeat what you desire nine times to yourself. On the ninth time, say it aloud and add:

> *Lucifer! You are my supreme lord, judge, and teacher! As I give you my soul, so fulfill my request!*

If the Horned One agrees, a red rooster will first appear at the crossroads and then a bear. Do not be afraid of them; they will do you no harm. After these visions, a demon will appear to indicate what to do next to fulfill the contract. Immediately do what the demon indicates. It is strictly forbidden to leave any actions for later, due to, for example, lack of time. All the requirements must be fulfilled scrupulously, no matter how strange they may seem. As a rule, one of the central requirements is the conclusion of a relevant treaty, which, of course, must be signed with blood at the end. After that the agreement comes into force, and everything conceived in the very near future will begin to be implemented.

✳ A CONTRACT WITH THE DEVIL

For mages of the highest degree of initiation, it is permissible to organize and conduct the following rite. Before carrying out the ritual, one should bring a fitting sacrifice to the dark forces. Then, with a special knife, the mage sculpts a rod from the wood of a never-fruited hazel tree. This will be a special destruction rod. Next you need to go to some completely deserted place and start this secret rite there.

Light two ceremonial candles forming two bottom points of a triangle. Stand at the apex of the triangle with the destruction rod in one hand and the contract in the other. Then pronounce a special spell to summon the spirit of hell. Many experienced and enlightened mages have their own unique and already tested spell. If you want to be seriously engaged in magical practices, you cannot avoid constant interaction with these dark forces.

The request should explain exactly what it is for and also the nature of the contract itself. It is the demon, however, who decides how to act toward such requests. In some cases, the devil can leave them without paying any attention, simply considering one or another mage unworthy. In other cases, if he is angry, he may simply destroy the mage. You need to be prepared for any outcome of this venture once you choose to undertake it.

12

THE THIRTEEN VERETNIC SPELLS OF EVIL

Note: These thirteen powerful spells can be performed in any order.

✣ THE FIRST SPELL OF EVIL

This spell helps the aspiring Veretnic or mage to establish his or her power. Gather all the church items in your dwelling, including a crucifix. Next, burn all these items on the waning moon and bury the ashes at a crossroads in the countryside.

Go to a cemetery on the full moon, taking a coin, a knife, and an icon of the holy trinity. Greet the mistress of the cemeteries and offer her the coin. When you reach the first crossroads of the cemetery, face west and, while holding the knife in your right hand and the icon in your left, recite the following curse once.

> *I am a Veretnic. The recently departed will now serve the forces of the damned. I summon them. I cry out, and with this cry I open the doors forged by these forces. I call the fierce and wicked power. With a lustful curse, I open a path in the minds of the righteous to the Unclean Forces. I beckon to them, and if they stray from the path, they will face cruel torment. Nema!*

Afterward hold the icon in your teeth and use the knife to spill a little bit of blood from a finger of your left hand. Smear a drop of blood on your forehead, then split the icon in half and scatter the pieces to the left and the right. You must not wipe the blood from your forehead, and you must leave without looking back.

✳ THE SECOND SPELL OF EVIL

This second powerful spell is for condemning an enemy to torments and a violent death. At midnight, sit down at a table covered with a black tablecloth. Put a holy icon with the same name as your enemy in front of you and a cursed icon between you and the holy icon. Place two black candles on either side and light them. Holding a knife in your right hand, trace, with the point of the knife, a circle around the candles and icons while reciting Satan's prayer once.

> *I believe in Satan, the Great Prince, the Almighty, and in the demons of the Great Prince, and all who are born in heaven and are fallen from heaven. From them the great truth is born, and it is indefatigable (never ending, infinite), forever and ever. May they reign on the throne of God and grace will come forever, for the children of Satan, not for those who pray to god and the holy spirits. May all the depths of the hell be sanctified, but all the devils on thrones and the princes will sit, yes to rule forever, and the people who are dark in honor and glory will live forever, Satan's grace, and eternal life will be tidy. And the people of God and the priests in hell will always be with the angels of God and God themselves. Nema! Nema! Nema!*

Then say the second curse of evil thirteen times in a row.

> *Prince Satan, you are master of my flesh, which is not humble, and my black soul. Come to me and help me to slay my enemy and lead him to a violent death. I'm a Veretnic. I am faithful to*

you and lead the people of God to your side. I lead your army,
full of strength. Let those who dare disobey rot to death, and let
me bring the lustful to their fatal ruin. You will rise, Satan, to the
high hill of heaven, to take your place on the throne. The Heavenly
Father will fall with the angels, and people obedient to hell will do
away with him. You will begin to reign over us with grace. So help
me, a Veretnic, in my wickedness and let [name] begin to suffer
and rot. Let [name] face cruel torment. Let the worms begin to
fester in [name's] flesh, let him/her writhe in his/her grave. Nema!
Nema! Nema!

Afterward use your knife to scratch out the icon's face. Snuff out all the candles, and bury the icon face down in damp ground at the enemy's home.

⁑ The Third Spell of Evil

This spell will bring physical and psychological pain and torment to an enemy. At midnight, put icons of the damned on a table covered with a black tablecloth. Place black candles on each side. Light the candles and put an icon of the holy adversary before one of them. Using a ritual knife, heat the blade over one of the candles and say thirteen times in a row:

I summon the forces of the damned from the depths of hell. I cry
out for the evil of this overwhelming force. Let it form into an arrow,
and with a bolt of lightning cast it upon [name]. The fervent blow
will pierce [name], and his/her insides will bend and break. It will
tear [name] to pieces and bury him/her in the ground. It will drag
[name's] soul to hell, and there [name] will be ripped apart. On
the thirteenth night, [name] will be tormented by grief. No one will
break my word or reverse my deed. Nema! Nema! Nema!

Pierce the face of the saint with the cursed knife, and then leave the knife on the enemy's doorstep.

✳ THE FOURTH SPELL OF EVIL

This spell is used to bind two people together. Take a crucifix from a church. At midnight during the full moon, walk in the forest until you reach the crossroads of a trail and place the crucifix on the ground, face up to the sky. Say the following nine times, while you trample the crucifix and wipe off your boots on it.

> What the holy church created, I trample and stomp, mixing it with the earth, the dust, and the dirt. The power of Christ will descend into filth. Demons will rejoice and rise up from the depths of hell. For this blasphemy, I ask the forces of the damned to pull, draw, and bind [name] to [name] so that they will live together. If he leaves her for another, tragedy will strike him, and he will not live another day without her. Nema! Nema! Nema!

Turn the crucifix face down in the dirt. Sprinkle dirt over it and leave.

✳ THE FIFTH SPELL OF EVIL

Take a holy icon and a knife, and on the night of the full moon, go into the forest. Place the icon, cut in half with an ax, on a stump, and say nine times in a row:

> As I give a holy icon cut in two to the demon for his enjoyment, so let him send an arrow into the heart, head, and veins of [name]. Let the arrow strike [name's] flesh and his mind from now on so that [name] will become a slave. Torment [name] day and night with passion and love, let him look for her, search for her in his mind, stalk after her. Day and night, he will be unable to rest from his lust for her. He will shake and thunder from the need to quench his passions. He will follow after her like a dog and never stray from her even a step. Nema! Nema! Nema!

Bury the broken icon under the stump and leave. Take a pinch of ground from the place where you buried the icon and scatter on four sides at the crossroads.

✿ THE SIXTH SPELL OF EVIL

In this spell an icon of the holy trinity is sacrificed to a spirit to whom you are faithful. Go to a crossroads at midnight, holding a bewitched knife in your right hand and a hated holy icon in your left. Facing west, say once:

> *I call the forces of the damned from the depths of hell. I destroy the icons of the foul holy people without shame and ask for the grace of demons. I ask for the strongest demons to act as my shields so that I may be protected from all sides. I defend myself neither with fire nor with a sword. No one will reach me, as a demon will guard me for all eternity. Nema! Nema! Nema!*

Cut the icon in half with the knife. Gather dirt from under your feet, put it in a bag, and carry or wear the bag near your chest.

✿ THE SEVENTH SPELL OF EVIL

This is a spell for inflicting illness on an enemy. Take an icon from the enemy's church. At midnight when the moon is waning, place the icon in a hole at a churchyard crossroads. Stand facing west and say once:

> *Forces, I am a Veretnic, and a loyal servant to you and your assistants. You have been feeding on people's souls. Now I ask that you give [name] a festering illness. I ask you, wicked spirits, and so do not refuse me. I need you to help me draw [name] to this place and bury [name] in this earth. As I see your holy visage, and you are the one who records, notices, and notes, bring [name] here within forty days. Nema! Nema! Nema!*

Take out the icon, scratch the sign of Death on it with a knife, return it to the hole, cover it with dirt, and leave.

✳ THE EIGHTH SPELL OF EVIL

This spell sends a plague to the home of an enemy. Gather dirt from thirteen graves of elderly people in exchange for coins. Destroy a holy icon until it is nothing more than dust and put everything into a pot. Cut off the head of a black rooster and spill the blood into the pot. Light a fire underneath. Take a feather from the rooster and use it to stir the mixture counterclockwise. Say:

> By the demons themselves, a secret has been foretold at forty
> pathways for all of my life. I come to appeal to the force today.
> As I come and bow to you, so I ask for your aid. You, the force
> of the damned of the cursed deed, I ask that you set a plague on
> the home of [name], as I praise you. I ask that you help me in my
> deed. Nema! Nema! Nema!

Pour out the mixture on the enemy's threshold.

✳ THE NINTH SPELL OF EVIL

This spell calls on the forces of the damned for good fortune and riches. Find a tree that resembles Christ's Crucifixion in the forest. Take an ax and cut it in two with a single strike, leaving a stump. Place something representing the hated trinity (God, Jesus Christ, Holy Spirit) on the stump, and set the trunk on top of it. Say the following:

> With an ax I cut the hated one and praise the demon who has a
> century's good fortune that he may transfer that good fortune, the
> luck of the forces of the damned, to me for my blasphemy. I will be
> rich and full if each moon I cut an icon with my ax and knife. If I do
> this I will not do so on credit, going around the world. I'll back my
> word with an ax and my curse with an oath. Nema! Nema! Nema!

Take a pinch of earth from under the stump, put it on your tongue, swallow it, and leave.

❊ THE TENTH SPELL OF EVIL

Use this spell to gain the aid of the demon Herod. You will need: icons of the demon mother and of Herod, forty church candles, a black candle, a baby chicken, a mirror, and a black rag.

At midnight, when the moon is full, place the two icons on a table covered with a black tablecloth. Arrange forty church candles around the icons, going counterclockwise. Place a black candle in the center before the icons and light it. Tear the head off the chick and smear its blood on the mirror. Hold the mirror facing the icons and candle, and while the candle burns, say the following:

> *The demon mother gave birth to you, Herod, when she was a*
> *woman. Afterward she became a demoness for all eternity, when*
> *holy war fouled the world. I praise her, so do not refuse me.*
> *Present me with an assistant. Nema! Nema! Nema!*

As the candle dies, wrap the mirror in a black rag. At every full moon, cut off a chicken's head and smear its blood on the mirror. If you do so faithfully, the demon will serve you truly.

❊ THE ELEVENTH SPELL OF EVIL

To invite support from Cain, use this spell. On the full moon, take a lamb into the forest. When you come to a trail crossroads, slit its throat and let the blood drain onto the ground. Say the following:

> *Cain was born a half demon and became a cruel demon who*
> *gorged himself on Earth, felled his enemies with his sword,*
> *plucked out their tongues with pliers, brutally tortured the dying*
> *with burning iron, and crushed the women and girls to death. He*
> *lived so and glorified himself. He was a half demon who became*
> *a demon when he drank a draught with lead poured in. I, the*
> *Veretnic, nourish the fire bloods that I may nourish and honor the*
> *demon. Nema! Nema! Nema!*

After this ritual, Cain will always help you if you light a candle and say:

> *Cain, go to [name] and let him rot. Nema!*

Then burn a candle on the enemy's threshold.

✳ The Twelfth Spell of Evil

This is a general spell for drawing the power of the damned into your being. Burn a holy icon of the hated trinity in the woods at night. While walking clockwise around the fire, recite the following spell loudly and clap until the fire has almost burned to the ground.

> *With the fires of hell, I, a heretic, am defying the holy. I draw the power into my veins. I will let the spark of wretchedness live in me. I will help to create evil, and those who go against me go to their deaths. Nema! Nema! Nema!*

Leave in silence.

✳ The Thirteenth Spell of Evil

This spell sends blemishes, aches, and sickness to an enemy. In the courtyard of a church, use a knife to draw the seal of Abar, the church demon, on the ground. Enter the church with forty candles as small offerings on the eve of the memorial for a recently deceased person.

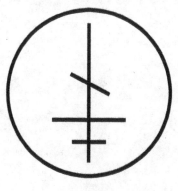

Seal of Abar

Walk around the church counterclockwise. Place twenty-seven of the candles upside down and whisper:

I do not wish [name] well but deprive him of his health. Abar!

Afterward place the remaining thirteen candles upright on the altar and continue:

Not in the name of the father, the son, or the Holy Spirit, but in the name of the forces of the damned, I am a Veretnic and with this blasphemy I send [name] blemishes and aches. I perform this blasphemy to cause sickness. I want [name] to experience this sickness, to waste away. Abar! Abar! Abar!

And then leave.

INDEX

Abar, 26, 157
Abrahamic religions, 18
Adam, 26, 41–42
Agrippa, Cornelius, 144
Alatyr-stone, 69–71
alcohol, curse to make person addicted
    to, 110–11
Amodeus, 26
ancestral mages, 11–12
angels, 7
animism, 18–19
apples, blood love spell on, 141
Arzhun, 27–28
Aspid, 29–31, 41. See also demonic
    pantheon
  background, 29
  control of evil spirits, 29–30
  Eve and, 26, 28, 41
  giving of knowledge, 30
  night of July 6 and, 30–31
  sacrifices and, 30
association, law of, 67

Baal, Alatyr-stone creation, 70–71
Beelzebub, 71, 117
belonging, 55–56
bewitched knife, 82–83

black books, 1
black icons, 17–18
black magic. See also magic; Russian
    black magic; sorcery
  best time for, 73
  concepts, 9
  creation of, 20
blood
  in black magic, 139–40
  energy and strength of blood, 139
  love spell, using, 140–41
  love spell on apples, 141
  ritual, methods of obtaining, 142
blood curse powder, 141
books of shadows, 71–72
braids, 6
breakup and divorce spells.
    See also spells
  to break up a couple, 102
  over two graves, 103
  use of, 102
Buddhism, 40, 58

Cain, 28, 98, 99
candles
  church, use of, 91, 127
  for rituals, 91

Catholic Church, 144–45
cemeteries
  as city of the dead, 85
  days of reverence at, 92–93
  dead water, 92
  forces encountered at, 92–93
  offerings at, 86–87
  perception of, 85–86
  power of, 85, 86
  respect for, 86
  sewing in, 95–96
  transfer of disease at, 116
  use of energy in magic, 86
cemetery magic
  days of reverence and, 92–93
  grave selection, 87–89
  greeting/offering gifts to the dead, 90
  materials for, 91–92
  principles of, 85–93
  reciting spells, 91
cemetery spells
  breakup and divorce, 102–3
  to call/repel mages and others, 117–22
  curses, 103–14
  love, 94–101
  transfers in magic, 114–17
Chernobog, 20
Christianity
  before and after Russian adoption
    of, 5
  elements of necromancy and magic,
    21–22
  evil and, 7
  heretics and, 22
  "pray and be saved" and, 48
  Russian black magic and, 8–10
  trickery in, 53
church
  black magic rituals associated with,
    125

candles, using, 91, 127
love spell in, 132–33
mage behavior in, 125–27
reasons for going to, 123
removing sickness in, 132
rituals in, 126
sorcery, principles of, 123–27
time to visit, 124
church spells. *See also* spells
  daily black rituals, 130
  Easter curses, 128–29
  twelve infernal spells of heretics/
    Veretnics, 133–38
close the pathways, 108–9
contact, law of, 68
crossroads
  of abandoned roads, 148
  cemetery, spell at, 101
  defined, 74
  Devil's Cross, 78, 79
  as favored by demons, 78–79
  finding out who will die soon and,
    77
  as focus of impure forces, 75–76
  in funeral rites, 77
  illustrations of, 78–79
  as meeting places for mages, 76
  playful creatures at, 76
  power of, 74–79
  and protection from ghosts, 78
  sacrifice to the gods at, 78
  spirits of deceased at, 76
  suicides and, 77–78
  as symbol of triple epiphany, 75
curses. *See also* cemetery spells
  blood powder, 141
  close the pathways, 108–9
  death, 104, 107–8, 111
  defined, 103
  to deprive health, 112–13

for disease, 113
Easter, 128–30
with eggs, 114
on enemy's belongings, 105–6
fatal, 104–5
gravestone, 112
for illness, 111–12
to make person addicted to alcohol,
110–11
for serious illness and subsequent
death, 107
signs of, 104
strong curse, 109–10
transfer of, 130–32
types of, 104
white, ritual, 129

daily black rituals
love spell in church, 132–33
removing sickness in the church,
132
transfer of curse or illness, 130–32
Death. *See also* demonic pantheon
background, 33
brothers and sisters of, 35
characteristics of, 33–34
defined, 33
as force in the universe, 40
legend of, 34–35
as noiseless and unexpected, 35
offerings to, 80
souls of dead and, 37
death, of mages, 12
death curse. *See also* curses
defined, 104
gravestone, 112
signs of, 104
steps of, 107–8, 111
for suicide, 107–8
demonic doctrine, 18–21

demonic faith
beliefs of, 19–20
creation and purpose of mankind
and, 19–20
schools and sects, 19
tribal deities, 18–19
demonic forces, presence of,
22–23
demonic pantheon
defined, 24
Prince Aspid, 29–31
Prince Enarh, 32–33
Prince Enoch, 31
Prince Indik, 35–36
Prince Mafawa, 36
Prince Satan, 24–27
Princess Death, 33–35
Prince Veligor, 27–28
Prince Versaul, 28–29
demons. *See also specific demons*
black icons, 17–18
under Christianity, 7–8
conjuring, by name, 9
crossroads as favored by, 78–79
defined, 7, 8
home of, 37–38
how to summon, 83–84
names of, 7–8
as original dark gods, 10
revelations from, 16
roles of, 83–84
in Russian black magic, 9
"watchmen," 72
devil. *See also* Satan
as force in the universe, 39–40
pacts with, 143–49
repaying, 20
souls and, 43–46
spell to ask for power of, 121–22
worship of, 15

Devil's Cross, 78, 79
devil's trinity, 24
disciples, of mages, 11–13
disease
　curse for, 113–14
　transfer at the cemetery, 116
dolls
　composition of, 79–80
　for magical work, 79–80
　as puppets of the enemy, 79

Easter curses. *See also* church spells;
　curses
　forty days' prayer for the dead,
　　129–30
　for painful death, 128–29
　white curse ritual, 129
eggs, curse using, 114
eighth infernal spell, 137
eighth spell of evil, 155
eleventh infernal spell, 138
eleventh spell of evil, 156–57
Enarh, 32–33
enemy's belongings, curse on, 105–6
Enoch, 31
equality, 55
Eve, 28, 29, 41, 53
evil, spells of, 150–58

faith, 63–64
fatal curse, 104–5
fate, 43
fifth infernal spell, 135–36
fifth spell of evil, 153–54
first infernal spell, 133–34
first spell of evil, 150–51
5-road crossroads, 79
forces. *See also* Unclean Forces
　impure, crossroads as focus of,
　　75–76

spirits versus, 81
study of, 8–9
of the universe, 39–40
forty days' prayer for the dead,
　129–30
fourth infernal spell, 135
fourth spell of evil, 153
funerals, love spell during, 97

God
　characteristics of, 40
　in creating man, 40–43
　in creating the world, 40
　as force in the universe, 39
　in Judeo-Christian tradition,
　　48–49
　souls and, 43–46
　white-light teachings from, 44
good and evil, 4
goose, offering of, 115
graves. *See also* cemetery magic
　breakup spell over two, 103
　of children, 89
　choosing, 87–89
　of mages, 89
　novice selection of, 87–88
　performing rituals on, 90
　sealing, against a mage, 119
　in spell for contract with a mage,
　　117–19
　suitable, for sorcery, 88
　unmarked, 88–89
gravestone curse, 112
Greek myth, 74–75

Haley, 32
health, curse to deprive, 112–13
heaven, 44
Heavenly Father. *See* God
Hecate, 75

hell
  circles of, 25, 33, 38
  as home of demons, 37
  as Satan's residence, 7
  threat of, 22
hell icons, 17–18, 20
Hercules, 75
heresy, 14–15, 22
heretics
  Christianity and, 22
  defined, 21
  teachings of, 21
  twelve infernal spells of, 133–38
  Unclean Forces and, 21
Hermes, 74
Herod, 26, 27
Herodian, 26
Hinduism, 19, 40, 74

identification, law of, 68
illness
  serious, transference of, 114–15
  serious curse for, 111–12
  transfer of, 130–32
imagination, 61
Indik, 35–36
infernal spells
  first, 133–34
  second, 134
  third, 134–35
  fourth, 135
  fifth, 135–36
  sixth, 136
  seventh, 136–37
  eighth, 137
  ninth, 137
  tenth, 137–38
  eleventh, 138
  twelfth, 138
Islam, 18, 40

Jesus Christ, 42
Judaism, 18, 48, 71

knife, ritual, 82–83
knowledge, law of, 67
Korzhak, 27

Last Judgment, 33–35, 45, 87
LaVey, Anton Szandor, 49, 50–51
laws of magic, 67–68
Lilith, 26
longing, spell to torment with,
  98–100
love powder, preparing, 141
love spells
  blood, on apples, 141
  at cemetery crossroads, 101
  in church, 132–33
  during a funeral, 97
  love spell, 96
  sewing in the cemetery, 95–96
  sexual binding, 100
  for suppression of the will, 97–98
  to torment someone with longing,
    98–100
  using blood, 140–41
  ways of casting, 94–95

Mafawa, 36
mages
  ancestral, 11–12
  assistants of, 10
  behavior in church, 125–27
  characteristics of work of, 9–10
  after Christianity, 6, 14
  church candle use and, 127
  churches and, 72
  defined, 3
  disciples of, 11–13
  faith and, 63

gathering of, 6
graves of, 89
life of, 4
natural, 11, 12
oral passing of tradition, 4
patrons of, 10
power of, 10
power of occult rites and, 43
practices of, 72–73
as prophets, shamans, and healers,
   5–6
as psychologists, 65–66
real versus fanatics, 16
sealing a grave against, 119
spell for contract with, 117–19
study of forces, 8–9
training by, 11–13
Unclean Forces and, 10
visit to churches, 124
magic
   blood, 139–42
   cash and, 67
   cemetery, 85–93
   defined, 5
   energy of, 3
   faith and, 63–64
   financial side of, 66–67
   imagination and, 62
   laws of, 67–68
   religion's intersection with,
      21–23
   rules of, 60–64
   secrecy and, 64–67
   will and, 62–63
   word usage, 4–5
magical auto-training, 62
magical recoil, 80
magicians, 4
man, creation of, 40–43
meditation techniques, 62

money, spell to get debtor to return,
   119–20

name, law of, 68
natural mages. *See also* ancestral
   mages; mages
   burden of, 11
   defined, 11
   spellcasters versus, 12–13
   training of mages, 12
   transfer of knowledge, 12
nema, 69
ninth infernal spell, 137
ninth spell of evil, 155

Odin, 49, 51, 53
offerings
   at cemeteries, 86–87
   defined, 80
   feeling while making, 80–81
   forces versus spirits and, 81
   gifts to the dead, 90
   types of, 80

pacts with the devil
   in fiction, 143
   as indestructible, 146
   in life of nontraditionalist, 145
   in modern era, 145
   paper catching fire and, 147
   preparatory actions, 147–48
   signing, 146–47
   skeptics and facts of, 145
   spell for contract with the devil,
      148–49
   as written in blood, 147
paganism
   defined, 47
   as not a religion, 52
   philosophy behind, 58

pragmatism and, 54
reverence and, 51
rituals and ceremonies, 49
sacrifice and, 57
Satanism and, 48–49
Slavic, 20
trickery in, 53
way of living versus goals and,
   54–55
worldview, 48, 52–53, 55
worship and, 48
worship of dark gods, 52
personification, law of, 68
photographs, 91
Pilate, 26
power of words, law of, 68
"pray and be saved," 48
pre-Christian faiths, suppression of,
   6–8
predestination, 43
Prince Aspid, 29–31, 41. *See also* Aspid
Prince Enarh, 32–33
Prince Enoch, 31
Prince Indik, 35–36
Prince Mafawa, 36
Prince Satan, 24–27. *See also* Satan
Princess Death, 33–35
Prince Veligor, 27–28
Prince Versaul, 28–29

ritual knife, 82–83
rituals
   basis of actions, 21
   in churches, 126
   daily (black), 130–33
   defined, 20
   elements of, 20
   materials for, 91–92
   pagan, 49
   performing, on graves, 90

for removing sickness in the church,
   132
in secrecy, 65
to summon demons, 83–84
Rod, Alatyr-stone creation, 70
roosters, 81–82, 84
rules of magic
   faith, 63–64
   imagination, 62
   as magical pyramid, 64
   mastering, 67
   secrecy, 64–67
   will, 62–63
Rus, 1, 9, 16, 18
Russian black magic
   birth of, 3–13
   blood in, 139–40
   Christianity and, 8–10
   dual faith foundation, 8–10
   introduction to, 1–2
   legions of demons, 10
   methods of, 1–2
   Satanism and, 46, 56–57
   theories of, 2
   tradition of, 8–9

sacrifices
   animals in, 82–83
   of roosters, 81–82
   Unclean Forces and, 81–82
Satan. *See also* demonic pantheon
   background, 24–25
   changing desires and, 146
   characteristics of, 25–26
   demon assistants of, 26
   faces of, 49
   meaning of name, 25
   in medieval tradition, 46–47
   as prince of the world, 19
   Veretnics and, 15

Satanel, 24–25, 27, 44

Satanic Bible, The, 50–51

Satanism
aspiration to self-perfection, 54
defined, 46
LaVeyan, 50
mankind in, 47
as not a religion, 52
paganism and, 48–49
philosophy behind, 58
pragmatism and, 54
reverence and, 51
Russian black magic and, 56–57
sacrifice and, 57
way of living versus goals and, 54–55
worldview, 48, 52–53, 55
worship and, 48

sealing all roads and paths of life, 120–21

seal of Abar, 157

seal of Asmodeus, 117

seal of Astaroth, 117

seal of Beelzebub, 117

seal of Cain, 98, 99

seal of Mammon, 119, 120

second infernal spell, 134

second spell of evil, 151–52

secrecy. *See also* rules of magic
as balance between mystery and needs, 66
law and, 64–65
necessity of, 64
rituals in, 65

self-hypnosis, 62

Seneon, 32

serious illness and subsequent death, curse for, 107

seventh infernal spell, 136–37

seventh spell of evil, 154

sewing in the cemetery, 95–96

sexual binding, 100–101

similarity, law of, 67

sixth infernal spell, 136

sixth spell of evil, 154

Slavic black magic. *See* Russian black magic

Slavic paganism, 20

Socrates, 57

sorcery
best time for, 73
books, 71–72
church, 123–27
concepts, 9
defined, 4, 5
suitable graves for, 88

soul(s)
devil and, 43–46
God and, 43–46
in hell, 37–38
mainstream religion's misconception about, 42
of righteous people, 45

spellcasters, 12–13

spells. *See also* curses
action of, 94
to ask for power of the devil, 121–22
basis of actions, 21
breakup, over two graves, 103
to break up a couple, 102
breakup and divorce, 102–3
to call/repel mages and others, 117–22
cemetery, 94–122
cemetery, reciting, 91
characteristics of, 21
church, 128
for contract with a mage, 117–19
defined, 21, 68

Easter curses, 128–30
ending of, 69
to get debtor to return money,
    119–20
love, 94–101
for protecting books, 72
ritual words of, 68–69
to seal a grave against a mage, 119
to seal all roads and paths of life,
    120–21
transfers in magic, 114–17
Veretnic, of evil, 150–58
ways of casting, 94–95
spells of evil
first, 150–51
second, 151–52
third, 152
fourth, 153
fifth, 153–54
sixth, 154
seventh, 154
eighth, 155
ninth, 155
tenth, 156
eleventh, 156–57
twelfth, 157
thirteenth, 157–58
spirits
evil, control of, 29–30
forces versus, 81
summoning, to the crossroads,
    76–77
stewards, 11
strong curse, 109–10
suicides
crossroads and, 77–78
death curse and, 107–8

T-crossroads, 78
tenth infernal spell, 137–38

tenth spell of evil, 156
third infernal spell, 134–35
third spell of evil, 152
thirteenth spell of evil, 157–58
totemism, 18–19
training, by mages, 11–13
transfers
defined, 114
disease at a cemetery, 116
of knowledge, 12
offering of a goose, 115
rite of wealth, 116–17
of serious illness, 114–15
tribal deities, 18
tributes, 80
trickery, 53
triple epiphany, 75
twelfth infernal spell, 138
twelfth spell of evil, 157

Unclean Forces
heretics and, 21
mages and, 10
sacrifices and, 81–82
Veretnics and, 15

Veligor, 27–28
Veretnics
black icons, 17–18
blasphemy and, 15
defined, 15
fierce elders, 16
name, 14
obsession with desecration, 16
as powerful and dangerous, 16
Satan and, 15
twelve infernal spells of,
    133–38
Unclean Forces and, 15
Versaul, 28–29

voodoo, 10, 21

"watchmen" demons, 72
wealth, rite of, 116–17
white ritual curse, 129
will
  in magic, 62–63
  spell for suppression of,
    97–98

witchcraft
  beginning of tradition of, 4
  defined, 3
  faith and, 63
  good and evil and, 4
  phases of the moon and, 19
  systems of, 3–4
witches, 5
world, creation of, 40

ABOUT THE AUTHOR

Natasha Helvin is a writer, a hereditary witch, an occultist, and a priestess in Haitian vodou. An avid scholar of tradition and religion, she is also simply a woodland creature who feeds on folklore and magic!

Natasha grew up in the Soviet state, in a secluded small village amid dense woodland and endless rivers, until she was eighteen. With a deep-rooted connection to the natural mysterious world, Natasha inherited her passion for magic from her mother and previous generations, and she learned from her family the ancient secrets of magic and healing and the boundless potential of the human spirit. From this long line of metaphysicians and her rich spiritual cultural heritage, the roots of occultism and conscious thinking developed in her rapidly starting at a very young age. As a child she saw her grandmother and mother use magic in their everyday lives to assist neighbors, friends, and anyone simply seeking help. She spent a lot of her childhood searching for wild berries in the underbrush, "befriending" ancient trees and forest spirits, exploring ruins covered in moss and ivy—elements that unsurprisingly Natasha blends into her magical work and are still present today.

Guided by her passion, Natasha loves exploring the magical practices of ancient cultures and civilizations all over the world. She is a seasoned traveler—a globe-trotting pilgrim seeking out knowledge with every new excursion. From her far-reaching international voyages, she has cultivated an exquisite and powerfully integrated personal practice, which takes inspiration from the best and most sacred of the world's knowledge base of cosmopolitan and rural conjuring. Natasha expertly combines the rustic, pastoral folk wisdom of the old world with the modern pragmatism of today.

Natasha's lifelong passion is to share her practical, time-tested knowledge of real sorcery with people looking for alternative paths to self-empowerment and success. Her innate talents for manifestation and the hands-on application of conjuring and witchcraft have always defined her goals and vocational pursuits.

Natasha's goal is to share her knowledge of witchcraft with those determined to get more out of their lives. She is convinced that our physical senses and carnal pleasures, our human needs for luxury and tactile pleasure, and true wealth and success are all part of our human reality. We all want to be happy, healthy, wealthy, wise, and powerful, and we want and can create this reality for ourselves.

Natasha prefers the more intense side of conjuring. She excels at the magic of influence and persuasion, relationship spells, and the most intense forms of spiritual management and control. Clients seek out Natasha for her unique spells, skills, and power—as well as her wise and sagacious counseling. She opens their eyes to new perspectives and experiences that lead to long-term change.

She can help you explore the wisdom and the Truth of the Old Ways—of the original occult arts that are transformational and restorative—to lead a more rewarding life, having been fulfilled by the realization of your own powers and your ability to disturb the universe to bend to your Will. Her website is **www.worldofconjuring.com**.